AMAZINGLY
SIMPLE
LESSONS
WE LEARNED
AFTER
50

AMAZINGLY SIMPLE LESSONS WE LEARNED AFTER 50

Uplifting Stories and Words of Wisdom for All Ages

Compiled and Edited by
William B. Toulouse

M. Evans and Company, Inc.
New York

M. Evans and Company, Inc.
216 East 49th Street
New York, New York 10017

Library of Congress Cataloging-in-Publication Data

Amazingly simple lessons we learned after 50 : uplifting stories and words of wisdom for all ages / compiled and edited
by William B. Toulouse
        p.   cm.
    ISBN 0-87131-952-7
    1. Aged—Psychology. 2. Aged—Conduct of Life. 3. Self-
realization in old age. I. Toulouse, William B.
HQ1061 .A53 2001
305.26—dc21   2001033597

Book design and typesetting by Rik Lain Schell

Printed in the United States of America

9 8 7 6 5 4 3 2 1

CONTENTS

Chapter Three—MATTERS OF FAITH

Chapter Four—SETTING AN EXAMPLE

Chapter Five—JUST FOR FUN

Chapter Eight—SPECIAL VIEWS

Chapter Nine—AFTER-50 WISDOM

ACKNOWLEDGEMENTS

First, I want to thank the many fifty-plussers who took the time to share with us their personal learning stories. As every submission was straight from the heart and intended to help others, all the contributors deserve the highest honors. You will find their names and short biographies in the back of this book. Many additional names should be on the list of writers for passing along their valuable wisdom, but space limitations caused their stories to be omitted.

Next, I am grateful to the following people for their generous contribution of time and talent which made the creation of this book possible:

The selection panel was particularly important in that they had the vital and difficult task of reviewing and rating the many stories, poems and clippings that were submitted for inclusion in our collection. Helping to make the final selections were Jim Atkins, Lake Worth, Florida; Mary Dannettell, Evansville, Indiana; Mitzie Hankins, Huntington, West Virginia; Mary Lou Krueger, Fort Walton Beach, Florida; Ruth Lang, West Palm Beach, Florida; Homer and Shirley Nienhaus, Manchester, Missouri; Mary Ruth Oakley, Evansville, Indiana; Lisa Pinder, Royal Palm Beach, Florida; Robert J. Simonds,

Carbondale, Illinois; and Julian Ann Tunnell, Fallbrook, California.

Mary Lou Krueger earned extra laurels for lending her considerable editing skills to our project and doing so with enthusiasm from beginning to end.

Special thanks go to newspaper columnist and author Bard Lindeman, of Stone Mountain, Georgia, for his support and professional advice, and to Berlitz language schools instructor Freda Mills for her perceptive reading, editing, and evaluation of stories.

Again, I thank all of you!

William B. Toulouse

INTRODUCTION

The uplifting stories presented in this book are not intended to be the exclusive property of today's "oldsters." Many sensitive readers well below the fifty-plus line will find the lessons and wisdom they impart inspiring, touching, and entertaining. This collection should put to rest the old theory that learning is strictly for the young and not for those of us who have advanced a bit in years.

Since turning fifty quite some time back, I am constantly amazed at the lessons I, personally, still learn from time to time. It's not an everyday thing, of course, but it is a recurring experience. I have learned so much from the many individuals who have contributed to this collection of stories. In reading the formidable stack of letters that were submitted, in many instances I learned (or re-learned) the different meanings of happiness, sorrow, love, hope, charity, kindness—and much, much more. I am truly richer for having had the privilege of sharing these emotions with the writers.

This project began when a seventy-plus friend, obviously filled with some inner-satisfaction, said to me, "You know, I learned something new today." That remark caused me to think, "Isn't that wonderful—still learning at his age." Of course, I shouldn't have registered any disbelief at all. His remark was simply a testimonial to another old saying: *Wisdom comes with age.* As author Helen Keller once put it, "Life is a succession of lessons which must be lived to be understood." Another writer observed, "Some believe that the things we gain along life's way may be more important than those we lose."

Earlier I had read a lengthy newspaper feature describing how retirees are going back to school and signing up for adult education classes in greater numbers than ever before. Many are going even further, seeking fulfillment by working part-time in community centers, schools, hospitals, churches, synagogues, and libraries. These people are donating their knowledge and improving their lives at the same time; making new friends of all ages, all denominations; and keeping an open mind. Their new learning-and-giving experiences are rewarding them with a forever young attitude that becomes contagious.

So, the quest for knowledge is alive and well—and expanding—at the upper end of the age scale. Some years back, W. Somerset Maugham commented "When I was young I was amazed at Plutarch's statement that the elder Cato began at the age of eighty to learn Greek. I am amazed no longer. Old age is ready to undertake tasks that you shirked because it would take too long."

As former publisher of 50 *Plus* magazine (now *New Choices*, published by *Reader's Digest*), I have made special note of the many media features we read in the press and see on television today dealing with the very real and serious problem of memory loss often brought on by aging. This caused me to ask myself why memory gain was not afforded similar attention.

After my friend's comment about learning something new, I decided to poll a few of my fifty-plus friends and acquaintances on the subject. I immediately found that every single one of them told me of some recent "lesson" they had learned.

I was surprised to discover that their experiences, generally speaking, dealt with matters or philosophy that were not at all new. Obviously, these friends were simply re-learning some of the basics they had been taught much earlier in life but which required some recent event or episode to crystalize the meaning in their minds. In effect, the "teachings" of yesteryear—at last—sank in. One friend learned, simplistic as it sounds, that it really is better to give than receive; another finally realized that patience truly is a virtue. There were no astonishing revelations: the lessons were amazingly simple!

The writers who contributed to this collection—all over fifty and some past eighty—are happy to share with all age groups the intelligence they have gathered during life's journey. Enjoy the ride!

ONE

NEW BEGINNINGS

'Tis well an old age is out
And time to begin a new.
—John Dryden

Color Me Happy

Rita M. Haun

Today, I am probably happier and more fulfilled than I have ever been in my life. I am a seventy-one-year-old grandmother of ten. I live alone with my dog, Tillie, in what most would call a modest home, but to me it is an idyllic haven. I have a lovely yard that I work myself. It is filled with flowers and trees, feisty squirrels, a great variety of birds, magnificent butterflies, and a few quaint benches and statues.

I grew up in an era and in a family where the most important goal for a female was to be a "good girl." You always turned the other cheek. You never allowed yourself to come first or even second; maybe fourth or fifth, and by that time you were too emotionally spent to know what you wanted. There was a neurotic insistence on perfection, a standard no one could live up to. Now I know that perfection is unattainable. Now I try to live up to my own standards and not the world's, and that is difficult enough. I no longer constantly give in to the needs of others by denying my own. I no longer ignore the careless cruelties of loved ones in order to keep peace.

My family is my dearest love and I try to be as generous with my time and gifts as I can possibly be. But now, at seventy-one, I feel I am entitled to come first once in a while. I take all the time I want for books I never had time to read. I have made comfortable niches all over my house that are great for curling up with a book. I have this wonderul freedom. I can eat when and if I want; I can turn on every light in my house or I can sit in candlelight; I can sleep or not sleep if I want. I can dabble in watercolors and feel perfectly satisfied with the results, not caring one bit what the world would think. I can wear comfortable clothes and shoes and not worry about my hair, or I can treat myself to the beauty shop and feel snazzy for an afternoon.

I've also learned that I have a lot of control over my mind and the things that happen to me. I can wake up in the morning and feel depressed. What I do with that makes all the difference in the world. I can think over all the wonderful things that I have, shake the depression off and make a wonderful day. Someone said, "You have a brush, you have colors. Paint paradise and walk right in." Or, you can very easily give in to that depression and create a hellish day.

My recently acquired computer gives me many happy hours. Needless to say, I went through more than a few frustrations trying to learn how it works. I have delved into history and literature (my two favorite subjects) to my heart's content. Sometimes, on the computer, I even take a break to enjoy a few games of solitaire. And I get e-mail from my grandchildren from all over the country.

NEW BEGINNINGS

From my dog, Tillie, I get unbelievable amounts of love and devotion. Because of her, four times a day, regardless of the weather, I have to get out and walk. Because of yard work and Tillie, I get lots of outside exercise, which I know is important.

I have never been an optimistic person. Far from it! I have not had an easy life. Some pretty nasty things have happened to me. Five years ago I even had breast cancer. But today, with my new outlook, it is as though God has said, "This time is for you!" and I am enjoying the novelty very much. I have painted Paradise and have walked in.

—*Lesson learned*: Changing the ways of yesterday can change your life for the better.

A Second Life

Marjorie Free

Looking back on the scene today, I can't believe it!

There I was on my bicycle, rolling along at a reasonably fast clip, a bit unsteady with a wobble here and there, but it was a new bike, so I had to get used to it. After finding I could navigate the sidewalk successfully, I was ready to venture into the street. Down the street I went, into the park and across the bridge—only to meet other cyclists speeding towards me. My fearless and persevering self instantly turned into a full-fledged coward and I sailed off the street and into a ditch. Fortunately, I was soon right side up and off again on my journey.

Just a kid headed for school? No, I was over fifty and on my way to my new job as a counselor in a Hearing and Speech Clinic. The bicycle episode quickly taught me that while I knew I could have broken every bone in my fifty-year-old body, my twenty-year-old perseverence was still very much alive.

All this was a new life for me. I had experienced a midlife crisis. Big decisions. Hard decisions. I divorced after twenty-three years of marriage—and faced the future solo. It was a scary time, and yet I was exhilarated at the prospect of fulfilling a dream or two.

I reentered the field of education and began taking

classes at the university nearby and working towards my
Master's degree. The oral presentation for the degree
came at last and, despite my age, I faced my committee
with an almost naive calmness. (Maybe wisdom does
come with age!) And so it was that I passed a significant
milestone in my new life. As a fifty-plusser I reveled in
the warm feeling of satisfaction and accomplishment on
the day I received my degree.

At that point I was totally broke and immediately
applied for the Hearing and Speech Clinic position.
Upon receiving my first paycheck from the job, I paid
cash for the new bicycle that I rode to work. It was a
great time of life for me: a time of freedom and new
vistas and new activities. It didn't take long for me to
spread my wings and fly.

One high point of this special period was when my
housemate and I decided to embark on an exciting and
enriching adventure together. We bought a motor home
(quite a step up from a bicycle!) and spent every weekend on the Oregon coast. It was during those days that I
learned the true meaning of the statement by author
Pearl S. Buck that "Life is never dull when he or she
becomes the creator."

—*Lesson learned:* You can do anything if the body has energy
and the mindset is determined. Now, in my seventies,
I'm slowing down a bit but still have that same spirit
I discovered years ago when I created my "second life."

Be on the Bright Side
Helen Troisi Arney

I couldn't find a listing for her in the phone book, so I decided to go directly to her home. Her name and address had been given to me by her Meals on Wheels deliverer who suggested I meet her because "she's such an interesting person."

My purpose was to interview Annie Flynn, an over-eighty black lady, for my column "Widowed Walk," which I wrote for a local newspaper. Annie opened her front door and motioned me in. "Sit down," she said, rather gruffly I thought.

All kinds of thoughts raced through my mind: she'll resent this white lady intruding on her peaceful day; she'll think her story is none of my business; she'll resist talking to any stranger. But as I interviewed her, she began haltingly to tell her story.

This little lady, less than four feet tall, had reared nine children; buried a preschool daughter and a teenage son; kept house in the pre-Pampers age when the dryer was a clothesline; raised and canned her own fruit jellies and vegetables; sewed for her children; and gave support to John, her husband of sixty-four years, in everything he did.

After putting aside my first fears, I noticed that Annie's round face could turn pixyish in a moment. She would admit that she was pleased with what she had done and felt she had "lived a good life." She felt blessed in having had children who helped at home and finished high school. She now has seventeen grand-children and thirteen great-grandchildren.

She and her husband knew each other sixty-nine years, from their high school days. Annie had been apprenticed as an undertaker but gave it up with regret when the babies started coming. John worked at an industrial plant and when the dollars didn't quite go around he also worked part-time at a local hotel and a local restaurant. He became a deacon in his church, where Annie helped with missions and eventually became president of United Missions.

She also helped at Head Start one summer, where, she said, "We taught the children how to love each other and share, and we read them stories." She could have had a career at Head Start had she not put John's wishes first. "I had it together," she said mildly, "but he didn't go for it."

John had died a year and a half before our interview, following an illness of only months. Annie was grateful he didn't have to be sick longer.

Those were the facts. What really impressed me was Annie's attitude. Diabetic and with a foot problem that has made her give up driving her car, she maintains that the foundation of her life is, "When you have Jesus Christ in your life, it's not a burden. If Jesus wants me, he'll take me, and I'll be sitting in this chair, napping."

Her life motto is, "Be on the bright side," and she repeated firmly, "I'm making it."

After I wrote the story, I took it to Annie to be sure I had all the facts correct. I offered to drive her if she needed a ride, a chore generally handled by her oldest son. "How much you gonna charge?" she challenged. There was that old, severe Annie back again.

"Nothing," I said. "I'd just like to help if I can."

We talked of many things in spite of the fact that her Meals on Wheels was sitting on her dining room table, and I worried that it might grow cold. She's a woman of strong, sensible opinions whose highest priority was her children's discipline. "I don't go for all this TV and e-mail for children," she said. "They dont make good men and women, and school can't teach everything. If you teach a child at home, he'll know how to act."

I was leaving when she said, "You in a hurry?"

When I answered "no," she drew me back inside for another fifteen minutes of chat. "It does make me feel better to have someone stop by to talk," she admitted.

I asked this wonderful mother to give me a hug, and she said, "I love you" into my ear. When I left, I wondered who felt better, Annie or I.

—*Lesson learned:* There is truth in the old saying, "Give what you have. To someone, it may be better than you dare to think." In this case, my gift of caring came back multiplied.

Change is Good
Kitty Marbury

With our newborn daughter, Ann, and her older sister, Sue, my husband and I moved into a wonderful new brick house on a beautifully landscaped lot in Baton Rouge, Louisiana. The year was 1955, and this was our dream home.

Many major events occured while we lived in this house, including establishing a business, watching our girls grow up, and seeing them get married and give us three precious grandchildren. I always thought I would take my final breath in this home—overlooking my garden in the comfort of familiar surroundings.

However, after my husband's death, I began to realize how ill-prepared I was for the loneliness that followed. I felt the need to be closer to people I loved. For quite a while I resisted the idea of moving. After all, my "dream home" had been my life and my anchor for forty-five years. It was a difficult situation, but I reluctantly decided to move a few miles away to be closer to my daughters and their families. With their help we listed my home and a beauty shop I owned with real estate agents, expecting the process to take months to complete. To our surprise everything was finalized in one week! Now I had to face the change.

My daughter Ann found just the house for me and, to my delight, it was in the hub of shopping areas, surrounded by good restaurants and, even more important, close enough to my church that I felt comfortable driving there. It even had an extra room, which I turned into a beauty salon where I could accomodate a select few of my former clients.

I found that my move was a positive one. I have "decluttered" my house and, thanks to help from my talented granddaughter, my new little cottage is quite the showplace.

One of the best things to come from this heart-wrenching decision to move is my supreme feeling of independence. I am now seventy-eight years old and feel younger than I did ten years ago. I still garden, drive, shop, and dine out in surroundings that have quickly become familiar to me. I have "started over" and have many new friends.

—*Lesson learned*: I discovered that change is good. My memories are not in that original dream home, they are within me—forever. And they, like I, have moved on.

If I Had to Ask

Barbara A. Kiger

I lost my sight when I was fifty. Suddenly and irreversibly, due to deterioration of the optic nerve, I was plunged into a world of total darkness. I thought my life had ended. Emerging after several weeks of vodka-soaked hand wringing, I crept out of my bedroom. Surprisingly, there was still a world beyond my closed door.

I remember groping my way through the dining room and living room to where my favorite chair had always stood. It was still there. Some things had not changed. Steeling myself against an avalanche of tears, I took stock of my life. I had my faith in God, though at the moment a bit tarnished, and a family who loved me despite the epithets I had hurled at them during the past several weeks. I could still hear, think, and speak. With that much going for me, surely. . . .

I wish I could say that everything was smooth sailing from then on, but it was not. Only after months that stretched into years of counseling and help from a pair of agencies whose mission was to help the blind did I regain my self-respect and achieve a modicum of independence. It wasn't until the day I was involved in a group discussion that I realized my true learning had just begun.

The group was mixed, male and female, some of whom I knew along with several I had never met. The discussion covered a range of topics, settling finally on the hot-potato issue of "right to life." Being a Catholic, I supported the church's view. It became abundantly clear, however, that several in the group were not of my persuasion.

Do you rememeber what it's like trying to interject an opinion when several people are expressing theirs? Watching mouths close, then jumping in is one way of doing it. When you can see, this is not a problem. Given my circumstances, however, this was not an option. Losing track of where the arguments originated because of the group's rapid-fire delivery made active participation even more difficult.

I felt myself being cut off from the conversation when, to my way of thinking, a particularly senseless remark caught my attention. Angered, I turned to my husband and demanded, "What color is he?"

My mind suddenly came to a standstill. I realized instantly that the question I had asked was no better—it was much worse—than the remark that had precipitated it. I tuned out my husband's answer. I no longer wanted to hear it. If I had to ask, was it really that important? As difficult as it was to admit, it was not.

—*Lesson learned*: I was freed at last from judging a book by its cover, or a person by the color of his skin. Now the world I live in is filled with new ideas and even newer friends. Too bad it took the loss of my vision to help me "see" what I had not seen before.

Coping with My Retiree
Lillian Jane Cook

My husband "Cookie" and I were driving along when it seemed to me that the car was gradually slowing down. Knowing what might be going through his mind, I said, "Honey! If you want to look at that old car back there, just turn around and take a look." Of course, that was all the encouragement he needed.

We were soon owners of a 1923 Graham Brothers hearse from Cuba, Kansas. It was hardly used but in need of TLC, which the recently-retired Cookie was eager to start providing. The "car" would be delivered to our carport in Topeka, the very place I had just filled with flats of seeds to begin a garden. The carport, attached to the free-standing garage and opening off the alley, would be great shelter for the "renewing" project.

Time passed. Every bolt, washer, hubcap, and engine part was meticulously inspected, polished, and replaced if necessary. The new headliner, upholstery, door latches, window weights, windshield wiper—even the 20-mph speed limit brass plate—gleamed. New tires were the finishing touch.

Before all this activity came about, our two daughters and I had been looking forward to taking our vacation time to visit relatives in Scotland and explore our roots there. Dad's mother and father, both named Scott, came to America by way of the St. Lawrence Seaway on different ships, met, married, and lived in Waucoma, Iowa. Later, the family relocated after the land was dispersed in an elder's will. We hoped to locate the Scott families of Dumphries and Glasgow by running an ad in the newspaper in Dumphries.

But Cookie had the car to see about. No travel was important enough to entice him away from the Graham. His devotion was kindled by his love and knowledge of woodworking and drafting, plus forty-three years of teaching shop classes in high school.

Disappointed and angry with my husband over my "lost" vacation, I turned to other interests. Along with these distractions, I enrolled in a Washburn University workshop given by the Menninger Clinic to "find myself." The process included answering questions, recording pulse rates, monitoring metabolism, wearing a small bracelet, and checking on the things which irritated me. At the very last session I was appalled to discover that my whole problem was me. I was simply out of sync with my husband: he was who he was and I had chosen a life with him. No one had ever told me married life was a bowl of cherries, and here I am upset with a man who is enthusiastic about an automotive restoration project.

The forty-five dollars I paid for the course was the best check I ever wrote. It changed my hurt to a taste of happiness with the man I loved.

Yes, we did get to visit Scotland later and were told, "You have brought the best weather we have had all year!" We met five delightful families in our clan and our timing was perfect to witness and marvel at all the huge hydrangea bushes in bloom.

—*Lesson learned:* I now look within myself before making judgments. I could have saved myself and my "Cookie" a sad time in our lives if I had just gotten smarter earlier—but better late than never!

Welcome the Sunrise
Mary Bordan

At age fifty-four, I was diagnosed with breast cancer, and I was devastated.

I had a small secretarial service in a section of my husband's locksmith shop in Melbourne, Florida. This was in the days before computers and color copiers and all the time-saving equipment used today. Folks would drop in with requests for a neatly typed letter to a Congressman, a government agency, or maybe Medicare.

My customers included older retirees needing correspondence about their pensions or young adults needing resumes for job searches. I fell in between these two age groups and worried about the future of Social Security, and how my husband and I would survive when we could no longer work.

We were managing to pay our bills, but there was never anything left over for an IRA, 401k, or even a savings bond. I felt there was no good quality of life after age fifty.

On the day our family doctor told me I should see a surgeon about possible breast cancer, these distant financial worries dimmed by comparison. My husband and I talked it over and decided I should have whatever was needed as soon as possible. I was in a daze but finished the work I had promisd my customers and advised them that I would not be at my desk for awhile.

My husband drove me to the hospital and I don't remember much more. When I woke up following the surgery, I realized that the worst had happened to me— a radical mastectomy.

After a number of blood transfusions I was still unable to walk or even sit up. I vaguely remember a priest visiting me one day and that night I thought I could see angels floating around my bed. The following morning I began to feel there might be some hope for me. I soon forgot the pain and despair I had endured, but clearly remembered the angels.

Several days later I returned home, weak but deter- mined to get back to work in my own little office. Radiation treatments left me debilitated but I graduated to hormone therapy and slowly but steadily improved. During this process I came to realize that in previous years I had spent too much time worrying about what "might" happen in the future and how we "might not" be able to handle it. I should have spent that time being thankful for how fortunate we were to have a generally pleasant life. Worry did not solve anything.

I worked for ten more years before retiring. I am now seventy-four and it has been more than twenty years since my surgery. I am not cured but I am doing well and enjoying a full life. I feel these are the best of all my years.

I get out early every morning and welcome the sunrise. I walk around my backyard and take pleasure in checking my orange trees and flowers. I appreciate each day and find myself observing things I had never noticed before. I ride my bicycle around the neighborhood and wish everyone I see a good morning. I am sewing quilts and creating gifts for friends and relatives to have something of me to remember.

—*Lesson learned*: Stop creating "might be" problems of the future. Live today. I try to set an example for younger people and help them realize that there is a lot of good and meaningful life to enjoy after fifty.

Happy Birthday to Me
Jean Vaughan

As I looked out that mid-February morning, it was over-cast and snowing heavily—and I felt as lonely and bleak as the winter landscape. When I started to turn from the window, I saw an elderly lady crossing the icy street carrying a huge load of groceries. Suddenly she slipped and fell, groceries flying everywhere.

Hastily grabbing a jacket, I raced out my front door into the street. Helping her to her feet, I began asking, "Are you all right? Can you walk? Do you want to come inside and sit down?"

When I shut up long enough to let the poor woman speak, she assured me she was fine, but would appreciate some help in gathering up the scattered groceries. We found that none of her purchases was too badly damaged and we repacked the bags.

This unexpected activity caused me to forget my feelings of loneliness and the fact that it happened to be my fifty-first birthday. The previous year, one month short of my birthday I'd lost my beloved husband of thirty-three years. After that day, I was completely lost: I'd spent my whole life being a wife, mother, and homemaker and had no idea of how to cope with being on my own. My three grown children were married and had families. I felt unneeded and filled with self-pity.

I quickly insisted on helping the lady carry her bags the short distance to her apartment. She told me her name was Dorothy, and she graciously invited me in to shake off the snow and rest for a moment.

She settled me into a chair at her kitchen table and began to sort the groceries. She explained that she had shopped not only for herself but for another elderly couple in the building. The husband was bedridden and the wife was unable to leave him alone. Dorothy also had picked up some food items for a lady recovering from a broken hip.

When I began to exclaim how kind and generous it was of her to be so helpful to these peple, she raised a hand to silence me. "I'm the one who is grateful to them for sharing their companionship and friendship with me. I needed it badly when I realized my personal problems were causing me to become uncaring and almost completely self-absorbed and isolated."

Following this experience with Dorothy (a special birthday gift!), I began to reach out and get involved again with people and to share, not only their problems, but their hopes and dreams. No longer steeped in self-pity and frustration, my life is happier, more fulfilled, and certainly more interesting..

—*Lesson learned:* "'Tis better to give than receive, for in giving you are rewarded tenfold."

From One Career to Another
Krystyna Mernyk

If someone had told me I would be canoeing on the San Juan River in Utah and the South Nahani in the Northwest Territories of Canada following retirement, I would have laughed at the very idea. For that matter, the thought of retirement itself hardly entered my mind even after I had passed what most people considered "retirement age." I had no desire to change my life.

My husband Ed retired from his job three years earlier than I did. He kept nudging me by asking, "When are you going to retire?" or "Are you planning to retire this year?" But it wasn't until my employer and I had a disagreement on my vacation time that I began to change my perception of retirement. I finally decided to call it quits.

I was surprised that my decision gave me a wonderful feeling of freedom. A whole new life lay before me.

Within a month I had enrolled with the local Cooperative Extension Service to share my horticultural experiences with young and old. This led to some writing for a local gardening column and participation in several garden clubs. I also became involved in volunteer work and various social activities—none of which I had time for when I was working full time. I happily found myself creating a new career. However, this one was minus the pressures and headaches of the old.

My environmental activism came about because of my canoeing adventures. I helped organize and lead fundraising trips for the local Sierra Club, and national and international travel became a bigger part of my life.

I have met many people who have become good friends and in my spare moments there are the grandchildren and family to enjoy.

I have been at my new endeavors for three years now, and I still love them all. I should have retired a long time ago!

—*Lesson learned*: We all have the power to take control of our lives and make the most of change. This power comes from us and not from others.

TWO

PERSEVERANCE WINS

*Give us grace and strength to forbear
and to persevere. . . . Give us courage
and gaiety and the quiet mind.*
—Robert Louis Stevenson, "Prayer"

On the Softball Field—Again

Charlotte Adelsperger

On a sizzling July evening I stepped into the batter's box, took a practice swing, and eyed the pitcher.

"Get a hit, Mom," my thirty-year-old daughter and teammate, Karen, called from the bench.

"You can do it," my granddaughter, Melinda, echoed from the sidelines

I took the first pitch—a little outside. When the pitcher lobbed the ball with a high arc down the middle of the plate, I leveled my swing and smacked it over second base. A solid hit to center! I heard ripples of cheers and clapping.

At first base I caught my breath and stayed put. An infielder tossed the ball to the pitcher. Myriad thoughts swept over me: *Here I am in my sixties playing on a women's slow-pitch softball team and I'm old enough to be mother to any of them. But I just made it to first base!* I'm glad I took the risk to play again—me, a breast cancer survivor, a victory lady.

During my teens I had been an avid softball player in a church league like this one. As the pitcher, I had helped my team win five consecutive league championships. It was "fast pitch" and I had developed my skills.

But now, over forty years later, when I was asked to pitch on this team, I felt very uneasy. It would take skill and concentration to handle slow-ball pitching. *Could I play well again? How would I look out there with veins showing on my legs along with other "symbols" of aging?*

Practice. It would take practice. I signed up my husband Bob to be the catcher during the week in our back yard. It worked. My confidence grew and I caught myself giggling like a young girl. I also found the strike zone.

So here I was in the game. One of my teammates hit a double and I scored. Soon the inning was over and I was back in the pitcher's spot beaming at a handsome young guy behind the plate—the hired umpire. (It never hurts to beam at the ump!) I faced batter after batter, and I got the ball over the plate. But sometimes my control slipped and I'd walk a couple in a row. I got tired, and perspiration trickled down my cheeks, but I hung in there.

During the seventh inning I was up to bat again. I knocked another single. My running felt like slow motion compared to the other players, but I made it to first.

"Oh my gosh, my mom's had a hit every time up. Three out of three! And we are winning the game," Karen blurted from the bench. I chuckled and danced around a little. Victory—and a chance to play with my daughter. It felt so good.

Someone asked,"How'd you get all those hits?"

"Must be the help of my trifocals," I said laughing.

—*Lesson learned:* My softball experience taught me how satisfying it can be to take the risk to get back into action (even if you are the oldest one on the team!).

PROFIT BY THIS

Katharine Hepburn, at age seventy-nine, spent an arduous weekend weeding and planting at her Connecticut home. This is how she summed up the lesson she had learned from her outdoor work:

"It was over. Now the job was done. It was night. I had had a bath and a swim and I was in bed. And I was thinking. You have now discovered the truth about yourself. Your parents gave you a great start. You were planted in good soil—fed—watered—carefully nurtured. And you were sent out into the world. And you were lucky. And apparently you have been successful. But have you accomplished all that you could have—given your beginning? No, you have been careless. You did not get to the essence of things. You can't do this and you can't do that, and you could have if you had concentrated and just stuck to it and got to the bottom of it.

"It's a bit late now, but profit by this—if you do it—do it. Get those weeds out. And plant carefully."

Move That Bod—It Pays!

Tony Jones

The Energizer Bunny—that little battery-operated drum
beater—could very well be a caricature of me. He and I
manage to keep running no matter what! Today, at eighty-
plus, as I look back on my life, I realize that my love for
exercise has kept me "ticking" through good times and bad.

I became a sports enthusiast in my teens and my
good physical condition probably saved my life in World
War II. I served with the Royal Canadian Engineers and
particpated in the D-Day invasion of France. I was later
wounded by a German Messerschmit but luckily recov-
ered and returned to Canada. There I immediately
resumed my various sports activities and have been active
ever since, competing in track and field events, javelin,
discus, biking, and golf. As the years went by I never let
up and never used age as a reason to slow down.

In 1979, at sixty, I entered the North American
Masters Track and Field Meet in Toronto and won two
bronze medals, three silver, and one gold.

At age sixty-nine I was honored to run for a distance
alongside the Olympic Torch as it made its way through
Canada en route to the 1988 games. In 1989, at the
Master Games in Copenhagen, I won the 400-meter
sprint for men aged sixty-five to seventy. But, unfortunately, shortly after this competition I was sidelined to

begin extensive chemotherapy treatment for lymphoma.

Nonetheless, in 1992 (I was still weak) my coach encouraged me (at seventy-three) to enter a race. I ran—slowly—but I did it.

At age seventy-seven, I realized a childhood dream: I had the privilege of actually carrying the Olympic torch for a one-mile segment as it was en route to the 1996 games in Atlanta.

While I have felt pleased with my agility in my "upper years," I was delighted and humbled in 1994 to meet two vivacious lady swimmers, both seniors, at a competition in Brisbane, Australia. They asked me if I would be competing in Portland, Oregon, in 1998, and I assured them that I was looking forward to being there. Indeed, we did meet, and once again they each won gold medals in their senior events: the butterfly, swan dive, and jack knife. But it was their words, not their victories, that have kept inspiring me to savor the rebirth of youth I feel in the sports I love.

"Will you be in Melbourne for the World Masters in 2002?" they asked.

"I'll do my best to get there," I answered.

"I'll only be 101," one of them said.

"I'll be 106," the other exclaimed.

And me? In that case, I guess I'll still be pretty young!

—*Lesson learned*: Always have an objective in mind. Keep looking ahead, and don't be afraid to break a sweat!

Fallen Leaf

Lanie Johnson

At summer's end, while I was working in the garden, a fallen leaf at my feet attracted my attention. I was fascinated by its unusual appearance and was compelled to reach for my sketch pad and begin sketching it immediately—almost falling in love with it as I drew.

As a freelance artist I have made numerous drawings, many of which were just plain, uninspired hard work. In this case I was not thinking at all of making a "good" drawing, I wanted to see and understand everything I could about the leaf, including its rips and holes and the soil it would soon become a part of. In the process, the leaf began teaching me about aging.

I knew that the natural cycle for a leaf is to emerge, fall to earth, decay and become nourishment for other growing things or beings. But this leaf's lesson was that if we take the time to look there is great beauty in all natural cycles. Later, in the fall, I noticed the subtle beauty of the tanzy after its flowers are no longer yellow but have turned completely black.

Following these observations, I realized that I had never thought of colorful fall leaves as *aging* leaves. This awakening was a rewarding gift to me. Since my early fifties I'd been trying to learn how to age, to be an elder without just getting older. Back then, while hiking in an East Coast forest, I passed a large decaying stump covered with fungi, and was struck by the thought that it was still a living part of the forest. Later, in Northwest rainforests, I was amazed at the many "nurse logs" with all kinds of seedlings, even large trees, growing out of them. I could see that the forest was still a part of them!

I was beginning at that time to see whole cycles instead of parts and pieces. Still, I had retained a firm idea that a person was very old by the age of sixty. A couple of months before my encounter with the fallen leaf (which was the only thing I "happened" to sketch out of a whole garden of flowers and leafy plants), I encountered my sixtieth birthday. Sure enough, I felt physically older on that day than I had the day before. I was even taking shorter steps than usual and I was afraid there would be a lot of things I'd not be able to do anymore.

Shortly after that landmark day, I received a calligraphy assignment and, despite over thirty years experience, I was actually beginning to doubt my ability to do the job. To my surprise I found that I could still do the work every bit as well as before, perhaps even a touch better. It was then that my confidence began returning and my attitude brightened.

And later, when I finished the drawing of the fallen leaf, I was thrilled to see that it was one of the best drawings I have ever made.

PERSEVERANCE WINS

—*Lesson learned*: There is beauty in all cycles of nature, including my own aging process. I'll keep remembering the fallen leaf—and draw more of those hearty "nurse logs" which represent the continuation of life, not the end.

Gonna Dance 'Til I Drop
Laurie Boulton

"Look at that lady," the teen exclaimed. "She can't dance." The YMCA wall mirrors reflected not only my image stepping awkwardly to "Boot Scootin' Boogie," but also three teenagers in the doorway laughing at my gyrations and pointing at me. I knew the boys were right. I was the only novice to sign up, and I became a frustrated beginner assigned to an intermediate class. I promised myself then and there that the words "She can't dance," would someday become, "Boy! Can that lady dance!"

For years I had yearned to dance like dancers on TV's *Club Dance*, but job, family and a busy schedule deprived me of the time I needed to fulfill my ambition. However, two years after my YMCA embarassment, my husband and I retired early and moved to Florida where we were able to pursue more leisurely activities.

Immediately, I signed up for a beginner Country Western line dance class. I repeated it twice, then moved on to an intermediate class two nights a week. Following that, I took a morning class to review dances taught at the local dance club. I observed styles and patterns of the better dancers and listened intently to instructions.

At last I was ready to hit the County Line dance floor. The simple dances came easily but others were a challenge. So, back I went to "remedial" classes.

PERSEVERANCE WINS

For months I practiced to be more fluid, programmed the dances in my head, then returned to the County Line. Yippee! I could keep up. I could dance! My best accessories were low-heeled boots and a happy smile. Other dancers and onlookers complimented me: "You're so smooth," or "How do you know so many dances?" If they only knew how many hours I had spent reaching that pinnacle.

At fifty-eight I feel great satisfaction learning new dances so "easily." I dance for hours while dancers watch my feet, which seem "Born to Boogie." I have endless fun, and so does my husband, who decided to join me rather than watch. We are now regulars at the County Line three nights a week. We dance longer and harder than most people. We work at perfecting skills and enjoy making friends. At the same time, we benefit from the aerobic exercise that is so vital for healthy hearts and so helpful in keeping us young.

There are moments when my spouse of thirty-six years thinks my creative engine is running in overdrive, especially since I began choreographing new dances. But he stays with me on the dance floor and beams when he hears, "Your wife sure can dance; it looks so easy for her."

I'm glad I make it look easy. A comment six years ago triggered an amazing inner drive for someone over fifty—and I plan to dance until the music stops, or I drop!

—*Lesson learned:* It's never too late to accept and overcome a challenge. Also, there are ample opportunties to remain active and energize our lives.

Oranges and Determination
Barbara Oeffner

One Saturday a young man came into the library where I worked. He smiled at me in a shy way and then, with a heavy Spanish accent, asked if we could help him learn to speak English. We had nothing in our collection that would meet his particular needs, but through our library system I was able to get a Spanish-to-English tape from another location. Victor Hugo Pool, the eager young man, practically wore it out.

During one of our early meetings, Victor told me that his regular weekday job at the time was picking oranges. "I work twelve hours a day," he said, "from seven in the morning until seven at night. I am determined to better myself."

To supplement the audio tape I asked a nun whom I knew if she would volunteer to tutor Victor one night a week, and happily she agreed to do so. This sped him along the way and he worked diligently day and night, never slowing down for a minute. Within a few months he was speaking English remarkably well.

In a short while Victor came to the library and excitedly told me that he had just taken a new job and was now a greenskeeper at the golf club nearby. "This is Paradise," he declared of his new occupation. "Thank you so much for helping me realize my dream!"

"It was you and your determination that did it, Victor," I answered him. "You kept your twelve-hour job, you worked nights, and you did it."

This experience caused me to remember a book I had read years earlier. The author suggested that we rate our tasks or objectives A, B, or C: A—very important; B—somewhat important; C—not very important at all. He claimed that most of us spend most of our time doing the C's and never getting around to the A's.

Victor inspired me. If he could do it, so could I. Therefore I started taking the author's advice, which was to spend at least five minutes a day working towards the A's. My premier A was to travel around the world and I put the five-minute plan to work on that specific goal. (Actually, I spent much more than five minutes a day.)

I worked on my world-circling plans, arranged a leave from my job, and was off on my trip. It was a wonderful experience, but it also taught me something important: we can do anything we set our minds to, as long as we work every day on our goals. In addition to my trip, I put these same principles work for other purposes. I finished writing a biography of Seminole Chief James E. Billie, and am proud to say it is included in our collection at the library where I now work.

Hardworking and determined Victor not only inspired me to make my dream trip, but to go back to school to begin earning my Master's degree. I am taking courses online, which permits me to continue working during the day.

Victor taught me more than I taught him!

—*Lesson learned:* Goal-setting works at any age.

Prayer

Dear God,

Grant me the courage of the daffodil,
To stand tall when harsh winds blow.
And make me brave enough
To hold my head high
Even when burdened
With late season snow.
And let me brighten
My corner of the world
With sunshine even
On a gray and cloudy day.

Amen.

—Jean Moyer

THREE

MATTERS OF FAITH

Set your affection on things above,
Not on things on the earth.
—Paul (Colossians 3:2)

Mr. Fix-It
Peggy Marteney

A frightening event took place one balmy Sunday afternoon when my husband, Gordon, and I were driving back to our home in Florida after visiting our daughter in South Salem, New York. We were traveling south on I-95 when somewhere near Brunswick, Georgia, we had a potentially disastrous blow-out. My husband, being an excellent driver, managed to stop our swerving movement quickly and pulled safely off the heavily trafficked highway. Gordon, in his seventies at the time, was not as strong as he used to be but, nonetheless, jacked up the car and proceeded to try taking off the wheel.

Cars and trucks went speeding by while I stood helplessly beside him vainly looking for a highway patrolman to at least summon a tow truck. After ages of struggle, there was one subborn bolt on the wheel that simply would not come loose and we were close to despair.

I am not an overly religious person and am prone to regard with cynicism other people's stories of divine intervention, but what happened next convinced me that we all have a guardian angel in one form or another. A deep voice behind us, seemingly from heaven, said, "May I help you?" Gordon and I both were startled and looked back to see the kindest stranger on this earth giving us a sad, knowing smile. It was as though he appeared from nowhere—we had neither seen nor heard him approach—but upon jumping up I realized he was indeed a mortal being. His shirt pocket was stamped with the name of a major auto service company, but he was with his family in his own car parked about thirty feet further back.

He worked silently and within minutes had the wheel off and the spare in its place. When we tried to give him twenty dollars he refused, saying, "I'll be repaid one day when someone comes along and helps my own grandparents if they run into trouble on the highway." In response I said that his was a beautiful philosophy of belief in the goodness of people, and my hope was that he, too, would be watched over by a guardian angel.

Gordon and I thanked him profusely and within seconds he was gone. He departed as quickly as he arrived.

—*Lesson learned:* The stranger not only fixed a tire, he rekindled my flagging faith in human kindness. (But, so our angel would not be required to work overtime, upon returning home we immediately bought a cellular phone!)

A Special Time of Life
Rev. Billy Graham

"What is the greatest surprise you have found about life?" a university student asked me several years ago.

"The brevity of it," I replied without hesitation.

As I have been working on this book [*Just As I Am*, HarperCollins], many of the things I have recounted seem as if they happened only yesterday. Time moves so quickly, and no matter who we are or what we have done, the time will come when our lives will be over. As Jesus said, "As long as it is day, we must do the work of him who sent me. Night is coming when no one can work" (John 9: 4).

In a similar vein, old age is a surprise to me.

"I've been taught as a Christian how to die," my longtime friend Allan Emery said to me recently, "but I'm discovering I haven't been taught how to deal with old age—with the time before we die."

Most of us when we are young, think that we are never going to get old. I certainly admit feeling that way from time to time. In the 1950s, I recall telling reporters that I doubted if I would live too many more years; the pace I was keeping was sure to kill me, I said. As I approached my sixties, I felt the same way. I knew I was similar to my father physically as well as emotionally, and he had experienced the first of a series of strokes in his sixties.

And yet as I write this, God in His grace has granted me

seventy-eight years of life, and I know my time on earth will not be over until He calls me home. I admit I don't like the burdens of old age—the slow decline in energy, the physical annoyances, the pain of losing loved ones, the sadness of seeing friends decline. But old age can be a special time of life, and God has lessons to teach us through it.

Certainly, one lesson is to remind us of our responsibility to be diligent in our service for God right now. I may not be able to do everything I once did (nor does God expect me to), but I am called to be faithful to what I can do.

Another lesson surely is to make us realize in a fuller way that this world is not our final home. If our hope truly is in Christ, we are pilgrims in this world, en route to our eternal home in Heaven. Old age should make us look forward with joyous anticipation to eternity. . . .

Over the years, I've had a number of illnesses and surgeries. Often they came just as we were about to embark on a Crusade or other project, and I could not help but wonder whether Satan was using them to attack our work in some way (and I suspect that was true). At the same time, though, God used them to teach me patience and to give me time that I might otherwise not have taken to read and contemplate. . . .

[—*Lesson learned:*] Suffering is part of the human condition, and it comes to us all. The key is how we react to it, either turning away from God in anger and bitterness or growing closer to Him in trust and confidence.

Detour
Ruth Wirth

On a summer vacation in 1997, my husband and I packed up our van and drove from our home in Florida to Nova Scotia to visit a close friend. The trip up was most pleasant and we enjoyed our short reunion, but on the drive back we experienced a strange episode.

It was a bright morning as we were nearing the United States border when suddenly, without warning, we found ourselves completely engulfed by a dense fog. Because trees lined that stretch of the highway, the fog made us feel encased by wilderness, and it almost seemed like we were in a tunnel; isolated from the outside world.

Although visibility was close to zero, we were able to make out the wording on a large yellow sign that loomed before us: DETOUR. My husband cautiously followed the arrow leading us from the highway onto a gravel road. At that point we pulled to the side to check our maps and get our bearings. We found to our surprise that this secondary road was nowhere to be seen. We thought of turning around, but there just weren't that many roads to choose from.

We examined the detour sign for any further instructions, but there were none. At the bottom there seemed to be the name of a construction engineer, but dirt and fog made it impossible to read. We soon determined we should follow the nameless engineer's urging and take to the side road—better safe than sorry.

We started off again, inching forward, our eyes straining all the while for the sight of a deer or moose crossing in front of the van, or some unexpected obstruction. Even with the windshield wipers on, we could see only a few feet ahead. It was so moist, rivulets made patterns on the side windows and, although it was morning, we had to use our headlights. Nonetheless, we kept moving ahead.

After what felt like an eternity (but probably was about fifteen or twenty minutes) we rounded a bend and, as if by magic, the fog lifted and we were astonished by a vast view spread before us. We could clearly see out over a lush, green valley and beyond to the Atlantic Ocean. In the small bay, dozens of picturesque boats and ships of various sizes were docked. A small village nestled on rocks that jutted out into the water, and waves crashed against the outermost rocks and the spray jetted upward.

We noticed one house in particular that had a bit more land than others. It had a garden, and along the drive there was a windbreak of trees. I was deeply moved when I realized that under each mature tree a new sapling had been planted—the beginning of a windbreak for the future.

When we had finished taking in this remarkable panorama, we observed another yellow sign noting that the detour had ended. An arrow pointed to our right, and as we drove off in that direction we were led onto a new superhighway—and headed home.

This whole morning adventure was filled with special meanings to me. I was reminded that when we find obstacles in our way, we must still keep moving forward. But occasionally in our daily lives we must consider setting off in a new direction or taking some route that has never been charted.

We need to help build solid rock foundations for our grandchildren and our great-grandchildren. We must nurture them like the saplings we saw, because they will soon become the sheltering branches for future generations. We must teach them basic values and pass along a firm belief in God.

—*Lesson learned*: We never know where the road of life will lead us, but around some bend the fog will clear and allow a new light to shine on us. The Master Engineer has helpfully marked the way!

The Schoolmarm
Catherine Berra Bleem

My husband, John, and I were both over fifty when the farm foreclosures of the 1980s began in southern Illinois.

Our dairy farm, along with others in the area, was targeted in 1984. We rallied a number of farmers who were in the same predicament and formed a group we called "Farm Friends." We prayed together, became amateur lawyers, fought the system—and lost our farms.

At that very same time, not far from us was a one-room schoolhouse fighting a battle of a different sort: it was being threatened with demolition by a strip mine. Named "Charter Oak School," it was built in 1873, closed in 1953, and now sat empty. The small building was eight-sided and, in its day, eight grades were crowded into the one room.

Each time I drove by it, reflecting on those bygone days, I wished I could have been a schoolteacher in the late 1800s. Although I had no formal teaching experience, the school held a strange fascination for me. I read all I could find about it and almost felt a part of it. I pleaded with God for its survival, and ours.

Happily, the school won its battle. The county historical society bought it and miraculously made it look new again.

MATTERS OF FAITH

Athough John and I had lost our livelihood, our prayers were answered in a different way, and we were able to endure. At first we rented a shoddy duplex on an old farm. John milked cows for a dairy farmer and after a short time found two better jobs: one as a part-time rural mail carrier and the other as a strip mine reclamation laborer.

During that period I volunteered at a small elementary school, and each year the first grade teacher there and I would take her pupils to visit the restored Charter Oak School. We would tell them about the old one-room schoolhouses in rural America and what school was like back then.

Two years ago, as we finished one of those school visits, a motorcycle rolled into the driveway. It was ridden by (I'm convinced) one of God's angels disguised as a tough-looking, skinny, toothless, tattooed man. He asked me where he could get an application for taking care of Charter Oak School. I didn't know that the historical society was taking applications for anything. He told me that he wasn't interested in the job himself, he just wanted to make sure that someone who cared got it. He fired up his bike and disappeared.

I immediately phoned a historical society member and asked for an application. A few days later, my husband and I were hired and given a very comfortable, two-bedroom mobile home at the school for minimum rent.

❦

Charter Oak School has a fascinating history, and my work there has afforded me the opportunity to meet, at least in spirit, the teachers and students of the past and to write a book about them.

Mr. Motorcycle helped me realize my dream of becoming a teacher. I am now known as the "Charter Oak Schoolmarm," giving tours and classes at the school—and I love it!

—*Lesson learned:* You never know who might lend a helping hand—or when. The motorcycle man helped give me a new life and proved to me that there is amazing power in prayer.

My Special Butterfly

Dolores A. Dietz

My husband, Joe, and I were having a leisurely morning, sitting around enjoying our coffee and talking. We had been married for forty-nine years and always enjoyed chatting about our family: six sons, thirteen grand-children, and two great-grandchildren. After a while, Joe decided it was time to go outside and putter around the yard. As he stood up, he said, "I think I'm going to faint," and he fell unconscious. The paramedics responded to my call in a matter of minutes, but it was too late.

Joe's and my faith in God was always strong and whenever we lost a friend or relative, we would talk about death and life after death. My comment would be that we have our faith so we should be happy for the person who has passed on. Nonetheless, I think we all have a little fear of the unknown, because nobody has ever come back to tell us what it's really like.

On that sad day I was reminded of my favorite story about the caterpillars. It seems there was a quarry full of caterpillars and they were always trying to climb up to the top. One day they all agreed that if any one of them ever got to the top, he would come back and tell them what was up there.

One day one of the caterpillars reached the top and

turned into a butterfly. He flew down all excited to tell them what it was like. "Look at me!" he exclaimed. But no one recognized him.

On the night of Joe's death, I got into bed and there was a bright narrow beam of light shining across the top of the dresser. I couldn't figure out where it came from or why. Then, a large shadow, like that of a person, appeared in front of the dresser. I sat up and it disappeared. I kept sitting up and lying down, but I couldn't make the shadow reappear. However, the light kept shining across the dresser all night.

The next night I got into bed and there was no light shining on the dresser. I finally decided the light and the shadow were Joe. With that realization, there was what felt like a hand that gave me three pats on the shoulder. I let out a loud sigh and said, "Okay Joe, I know it's you; you're here with me." There were three more pats on my shoulder.

With that reassurance, I felt so calm and relaxed. I knew Joe was a butterfly now, and he had come back to tell me.

—*Lesson learned*: I am now convinced that death is not an end and there is a God and a life hereafter. Our spirit lives on—and my Joe is an angel I call my "Butterfly."

LEARN TO APPRECIATE LIFE
Author Unknown (submitted by Carol Byron)

Dear Lord:
Even though I clutch my blanket and growl when the alarm
rings, thank you, Lord, that I can hear:
  There are many who are deaf.
Even though I keep my eyes closed against the morning light as
long as possible, thank you, Lord, that I can see:
  Many are blind.
Even though I huddle in my bed and put off rising, thank you,
Lord, that I have the strength to rise:
  There are many who are bedridden.
Even though the first hour of my day is hectic, when socks are
lost, toast is burned, and tempers are short, thank you, Lord, for
my family:
  There are many who are lonely.
Even though our breakfast table never looks like the pictures in
magazines and the menu at times is unbalanced, thank you,
Lord, for the food we have:
  There are many who are hungry.
Even though the routine of my job often is hard, thank you,
Lord, for the opportunity to work:
  There are many who have no job.
Even though I grumble and bemoan my fate from day to day
and wish my circumstances were not so modest . . .
                    Thank you, Lord, for life!

Believe It

Mitzie Ann Hankins

My son Eric was just a little boy when he was diagnosed with a heart defect. He had bypass surgery when he was six years old and did very well. He had a happy childhood and participated in sports all the way through high school and was seldom ill. He later married and had three children.

On an evening in May 1995, Eric, who exercised regularly, decided to go for a run in the park nearby. After he completed his run and headed home, he suffered a massive heart attack and died instantly. He was only thirty-two.

A short while later, my husband John and I were on our way home from a restaurant after having had dinner. John was driving and I was leaning back in the car seat looking out the window. As I often do in my mind, I was asking questions of God.

John and I were in our early fifties. I questioned the fairness of Eric being deprived of a longer life. Why did he have to be called away when his children were so little?

Many years ago I had been taught that when we die, we leave our physical bodies behind and enter heaven in a spiritual sense. I asked God if this is so, and if we are not physical, why do we need physical buildings in heaven? (I was confused because Jesus told us that in His Father's house are "many mansions," and there is room for everybody who is worthy of entering.) And since people have been dying for thousands of years and going to heaven, it surely must be crowded! The immensity of heaven must be more than we can even fathom with our earthly minds. Imagine enough room for all of us! Why would we need—and how could it accommodate—anything that would resemble material matter?

On this particular evening as we drove home, I did not speak to John about this puzzlement of mine. He had no way of knowing my thoughts and we had never had any discussion of what heaven may or may not be.

The next morning, Sunday, John woke me and said he had just had an incredibly vivid dream. In the dream he was walking down a street with many buildings of different architectural design butted against each other. He was shoulder to shoulder with throngs of people and he seemed to be walking a little below the actual street level. He knew he was in a big, beautiful city but he did not know what city. He was amazed at how clear and real the dream was and he could not think of any reason why he would have dreamed of such a thing. It was all a mystery to him and he was totally awed by the experience.

The dream occurred just before he awakened that morning and he obviously was excited as he described the details to me. I sat straight up in bed and told him, "I think that is a message for me." For some reason, John was the messenger—perhaps because we were both mourning our loss of Eric.

I accept John's dream as an answer to my questions. I interpret the dream as God saying, "Yes, indeed, there are many mansions. I have prepared a place for you—and your son."

—*Lesson learned:* God works in mysterious ways. Believe it.

Portrait of a Simple Era

Grace Lee Groves

I am now eighty-six years old. I was born the twelfth in a family of thirteen; nine brothers and three sisters. I'd say we were all born healthy, wealthy, and wise. My parents were Christians and taught us all to worship God and to love and respect each other.

As a little girl, I walked along with other children a mile and a half to a little country school called Greenwood. I had wonderful teachers and I loved school. When we got home from school, mother had just-baked bread waiting for us.

After eighth grade, my brother Marion and I went to Enid, Oklahoma, to Longfellow Junior High and stayed with my brother Howard and his wife. We would come home to Drummond for weekends. I had a wonderful year and learned so much: home economics, English, algebra.

At the close of that year we went to our church school, Miltonvale Wesleyan College and Academy, where I finished high school. I went back there for two more years and received a diploma in Theology. Without a doubt, those were the greatest years of my life! I met Fred Groves at school in Miltonvale and he and I were married in my home in Oklahoma.

Fred finished college in Alva, Oklahoma, at Northwestern College, and then earned his Master's degree at Philllips University. He was a teacher and administrator until his death. I worked at Bass Hospital as a nursing assistant for fifteen years while he was working in the Enid schools. After Fred's retirement and death, I retired also. Fred and I had a lot of enjoyment singing together for all kinds of occasions.

My faith and love for God have been the guiding star of my life, and I'm back at the farm home where I was born and have so many wonderful memories. Our three children, Carolyn, Roger, and Charles, were the delight of our lives—and they love me!

—*Lesson learned:* Looking back, I have learned that it was the solid foundation my parents provided for me— faith, love, and respect—that gave me a truly wonderful life.

FOUR

SETTING AN EXAMPLE

I bid him look into the lives of men
as though in a mirror, and from others
take an example for himself.
—Terence

Where Have You Gone, Joe DiMaggio?
Jean Moyer

It is morning. As usual, my husband Wendell and I are eating breakfast while we watch the early news. It was just announced that Joe DiMaggio, the great baseball player of the 1940s, had died at the age of eighty-six. I look over at Wendell, who is a lifelong baseball fan, and there are tears in his eyes.

This is not an unexpected death, nor is it a close friend or family member, so the tears are a surprise to me. I do not see my rock of a husband cry often. In fact, I remind myself, the last time was at his mother's funeral.

Wendell looks at me and says, "He was my hero. When I was young I wanted to be just like him. He was such a gentleman, and one of the best hitters and out-fielders of all time." Not being a baseball fan, I can only nod, and Wendell goes on. "I listened on the radio to games he played in and read about them in the paper. I followed his career all the way through."

It is apparent that Joe DiMaggio has touched my husband's life in many ways, and it occurs to me that the history of his childhood explains why. Wendell's father left his mother and his two brothers when my husband was twelve. Being the oldest, Wendell assumed the position of man of the house. He became the role model for his brothers and provided emotional support for his mother, who worked to support the boys. So it was important for Wendell to find a strong model for himself. Enter Joe DiMaggio. Obviously, this hero represented the kind of perfection a boy dreams about.

The press coverage of sports in the '40s centered on the game, not on the salary of the players or their personal problems, so Joe DiMaggio was presented in a totally different light than today's professional athletes. It appears that he never sought the limelight and was very much aware that he had a responsibility to the youngsters who were watching him.

Something sad has happened in our culture. In spite of technological progress, which makes our lives easier and more enjoyable in many respects, our perfect heroes today are few.

The story of my husband and his brothers has a happy ending. Two of the three boys completed college and went on to earn postgraduate degrees; the third had a military career and became a successful businessman. I can only imagine how much of a contribution the old-fashioned heroes made in the lives of these boys and, very likely, many others as well.

My husband's tears that morning were a sincere and heartfelt testimonial to the importance and positive influence of one man: "Joltin' Joe" DiMaggio.

—*Lesson Learned:* We need our role models more than ever. We may have to look more carefully; nonetheless, they are still with us. Perhaps off in some distant place, yet again, we might find them close to home— even across the breakfast table.

I Can Add Something
Lauren Bacall

Statistically I fell into the broken home category—
brought up by one parent, my mother. Through pure
luck—the luck of face and body, and having them
noticed by others at the right time—I was given the
opportunity to reach the highest of all highs at the age
of nineteen. Howard Hawks invented a personality on
screen that suited my look and my sound and some of
myself—but the projection of worldliness in sex, total
independence, the ability to handle any situation, had
no more relation to me than it has now. With that I was
also given a personal life fuller than I had ever dreamed
I would have, or, needless to say, have had since.

At the age of twenty I had grabbed at the sky and
had touched some stars. And who but a twenty-year-old
would think that you could keep it? When it all went—
though the career was more down than up almost
immediately—why did I keep going? Why didn't I fall
prey to the obvious pitfalls of life—booze, drugs, with-
drawal? I would say that being loved unselfishly by two
people had a hell of a lot to do with it. My mother gave
to me constantly. And her support, her nurturing of me,
her constant encouragement, together with the strength
of our family and my own character, my ability to laugh

at myself—all that is what made it possible for me to deal with Bogie [Humphrey Bogart], a man with three marriages in his past and twenty-five years on me.

And Bogie, with his great ability to love, never suppressing me, helping me to keep my values straight in a town where there were few, forcing my standards higher—again the stress on personal character, demonstrating the importance of the quality of life, the proper attitude toward work. To be good was more important than to be rich. To be kind was more important than owning a house or a car. To respect one's work and do it well, to risk something in life, was more important than being a star. To never sell your soul—to have self-esteem—to be true—was most important of all.

All this was so deeply implanted in me that I couldn't go down the drain. I am the sum of those two people and my beloved Uncle Charlie. Going back through my life until now, the Jewish family feeling stands strong and proud, and at last I can say that I am glad I sprang from that. I would not trade those roots—that identity. I have learned that I am a valuable person. I have made mistakes—so many mistakes. And will make more. Big ones. But I pay. They are my own. What was not real in Howard Hawks' [movie] version of me is not real now. I remain as vulnerable, romantic, and idealistic as I was at fifteen, sitting in a movie theatre, watching, being, Bette Davis.

I'm not ashamed of what I am—of how I pass

through this life. What I am has given me the strength to do it. At my lowest ebb I have never contemplated suicide. I value what is here too much.

[—*Lesson learned:*] I have a contribution to make. I am not just taking up space in this life. I can add something to the lives I touch.

Choosing the Right Path
Mary C. Dannettell

I began teaching school immediately after graduation from college in 1946, and continued until my retirement in 1986. It was a pleasurable but demanding and often frustrating occupation, and I often wondered if I had made the right career choice.

My time is now spent operating an antique business and doing volunteer work at my church. While these activities keep me quite busy, I nonetheless have time here and there to reflect on those many years I spent working with hundreds of students. I have learned that my decision to teach was not only proper but pre-ordained: God blessed me with a talent that I used for fifty years and the temperment to deal effectively with young people. The path I took enriched my life. I gave it my best.

I never realized earlier that I am quite frequently "rewarded" when former students recognize me after many years. I'm amused at seventy-plus to hear them say, "You haven't changed a bit—I'd know you anywhere!" When this happens I'm pleased and flattered but think to myself, "Come on now, I had to look better than this fifty years ago!" (It also reminds me of the saying that there are three stages of life: youth, middle age, and "you're looking good!")

Last summer I sat next to an "elderly" couple at a concert. After taking her seat next to me, the lady asked, "Didn't you teach school?" I looked at her closely and indeed remembered her. "You were in my very first eighth grade gym class in 1946 in Columbia!" I exclaimed. "Your name was Ernspiger!" We were both delighted with this unexpected meeting. Of course, we paid quiet attention to the concert but happily reminisced during intermission. Of course she, too, had put on years, but suddenly—even though ours was a teacher/student relationship—we were carried back to those special days of growing up together.

A man who delivered some roof shingles to my home not long ago said to me, "You were my gym teacher in the 1940s—I'd know that voice anywhere." And a month or two ago, after my picture appeared in the local newspaper in connection with the antique business, I received a letter from a girl asking, "Didn't you teach school? You were wonderful."

So, the rewards keep coming, like dividends from an investment, and I look forward to the next student recognizing me and saying, "You're looking good!" I'll answer, "You're looking good yourself!"

—*Lesson learned:* Give of your talents and give from the heart. You'll be appreciated—and remembered!

I Call Him "Angel Man"

Carole J. Cosentino

My husband and I were aboard a cruise ship sailing out of New York harbor for Bermuda when I heard a man repeatedly saying to anyone who would listen, "Hi, my name Emmet, first-time cruise." People were oblivious to him and I, myself, immediately tuned him out because he seemed annoying.

At dinner the first evening, we enjoyed acquainting ourselves with our tablemates for the week's cruise. I heard a very boisterous group a short distance away and when I glanced over, I saw that the gentleman who had called himself Emmet was seated at that table. I said to myself, "It seems like the man has finally found some friends."

The following evening, however, I happened to notice a gentleman with his back to me, all alone at a table for two. When I realized it was Emmet, I questioned our waiter as to why this man was seated alone. For some unexplained reason, he was replaced at his original table by a couple and Emmet was bumped! How cruel, I thought, and requested the waiter to ask Emmet if he would like to join us. Emmet was delighted and he was seated next to me. I soon discovered that he had a hearing problem as well as a slight speech impediment.

He explained how confused he was with the fancy menu selections and the waiter did not have the time to fully explain each entree—all he wanted was the basics. No escargot for Emmet! I offered my help and he was delighted with my recommendations and thrilled that he was trying something new and different.

By our introduction of Emmet at our table, he now felt accepted and eventually joined in the evening's conversations. Yes, it was his "first-time cruise" as he worded it. We found that he was retired and he told us all about his job at the post office, and his yearly trips to Hawaii to visit his only living relative, a sister. He was a delight and we looked forward to his company.

Since he didn't know his way around Bermuda, we told Emmet he could join us the next morning, and he was at the gangway, on time, with a big smile on his face.

Emmet joined us for all the after-dinner entertainment, but left at a reasonable time to give us our privacy. When we went shopping in Hamilton, he was right beside me, offering to carry my shopping bags. He felt accepted—and wanted.

One evening we made plans to go ashore to a cabaret show with our tablemates. Our cab, a beautiful old white Rolls Royce, pulled up at the dock and my husband suggested that I go with Emmet and two of the ladies in our group, and he would ride in the second cab. I was his "date" for the evening and Emmet made me feel so special.

During one of my strolls around the ship's deck, mid-week, I saw our tablemates talking casually with Emmet and introducing him to others. He was mingling confidently, and people were listening.

The last evening when we said goodnight to Emmet, he could not thank us enough for making his trip so memorable. He couldn't wait to tell his sister of his wonderful "first-time cruise." We said we probably would see him the next morning before we docked, but with so many people scurrying about preparing to disembark, I never saw him again.

—*Lesson learned*: He came into my life for a brief time and reinforced what I already knew: take time to listen; tune in to someone who is reaching out. Emmet is an "Angel Man" who tuned himself into my life, mysteriously tuned himself out, and made me shine!

A Thirty-Year Mystery
Marilyn Smith*

When I was a senior in high school I visited occasionally with a lovely elderly lady who lived in our neighborhood. I knew very little about her except that she was lonely and in ill health. However, her spacious and expensively appointed home indicated she was a lady of means and good taste. I had learned earlier from my parents that she did not have children of her own, which may be why she especially enjoyed my company.

One day she invited me to her home and said she had a gift that she wanted me to have. After we visited for a few minutes, she handed me a velvet case containing a beautiful, sparkling necklace. I was surprised and flattered but, being good mannered, did not venture to ask why she was giving it to me.

The next day I sent her a thank you note. The necklace was far too fancy and ornate for me, just over sixteen, to wear, but I could visualize myself someday wearing it to some extravagant party. A year or so later, I moved out of state and soon lost touch with most of the folks in my hometown.

I took a job at a hospital where one of my coworkers was Evelyn, a young unmarried mother with twins. We shared the same bus home and soon became good friends. On one of our rides I invited her to stop by my place for a visit.

Evelyn couldn't believe all of the "luxuries" I had. I didn't think anything about it because my furniture was used—I had nothing new to speak of. She told me that about the only thing she owned was work clothes. I fibbed when I told her that I had a problem: too many clothes in my small closet and dresser. Could she help by taking some?

Fortunately, we were the same size and in a short while we had gone through all my clothes and had put several pieces in a bag for her to take. She was delighted and it did my heart good that I could help her in this small way.

While going though one of the drawers we came across the necklace the elderly lady had given me. As I looked at it, I thought wistfully of my fancy party "some day" in the future. Evelyn was smitten with it's beauty, and for her, it was plain to see, owning this sort of trophy would be the impossible dream. I simply couldn't help myself and said, "If you want it, Evelyn, it's yours." She was astonished and couldn't thank me enough. In turn, I had never experienced such deep-down satisfaction as I felt when I saw her face light up. Again, my heart seemed to double in size. Unfortunately, not long after this I lost track of Evelyn when I made another move, but I never forgot that face.

Many years later, through a member of my family

and a member of the elderly lady's family, I learned that the 30 diamonds in the necklace I had given away were real, and it was not costume jewelry as I had imagined! It was worth a small fortune.

Had I only known, perhaps I would have sold it to pay for more training and become a nurse. As it is now—thirty years later—I continue to work as a certified nurse's assistant and I still wonder how much I would have gotten for the necklace and how much my life might have changed.

I also wonder what became of the mother and her twins and the necklace. Did she sell it? On the other hand, could it be that she, too, gave it away? I would rather think it helped her build a new life.

I will never forget her beaming face as she thanked me and said, "No one has ever helped me like you have."

—*Lesson learned:* Charity is rewarded in one way or another. I count the many blessings I have received since giving away my clothes and the necklace. And, if you are curious, the answer is, "Yes, I would do it the same way again."

*Editor's Note: Writer's name has been changed for privacy.

GLAMOROUS CHAMPION
OF FAMILY VALUES

Loretta Young, beautiful leading lady of film and television for over three decades, starred in movies with Clark Gable, Spencer Tracy, Tyrone Power, Cary Grant, James Cagney, Orson Welles, and Edward G. Robinson. Her NBC television series, *The Loretta Young Show*, ran from 1953 to 1961, and she appeared in 165 episodes.

Reviewing her career, Lena Williams observed in the *New York Times* that Miss Young's screen image suggested a blend of virtuous poise, sensuality, and vulnerability, and in fact, she once admitted to having had "crushes" on all of her leading men and being "susceptible" to men in general. In her 1961 autobiography she wrote that "A Loretta Young movie had a happy ending; that's what it was geared to: a nice husband, nice lover, no abuse of any kind—that's what the heroes and heroines were in those days."

Most seniors today will remember a trademark of her TV show: her glamorous entrance. "I did that to mollify the show's designer, Marusha," Miss Young said in a 1995 interview. "I initially just walked through the doors, and Marusha was upset because no one would see the wonderful back of the dress."

So Miss Young, who had studied ballet as a child, asked for a retake in which she entered the set and pirouetted before walking toward the camera. Viewers loved it.

Her show extolled "respect for law and order and for disciplined deportment and character-building standards," she said in her memoir, *The Things I Had to Learn*. "Above all, we wanted to prove the strength, the good, really, of people."

In her memoir she wrote of a lesson learned, a belief she obviously held her entire life:

"I believe that if we have lived our lives fully and well, and have accomplished, at least in part, the things we were put here to do, we will be prepared—mentally, spiritually, and physically—for our separation from this world."

—W.B.T.

My Father's Legacy
Lee Berk

It was 1946, World War II was over, my wounds were healing, and my Purple Heart was resting in a box on my dresser. I was once again a civilian returning to normal life in Green Bay, Wisconsin.

It was break time at work and I took my usual place on a stool at the counter of Ford Hopkins Drug Store. The *Press Gazette* was spread out before me as I sipped my coffee and read about my heroes, the Green Bay Packers. I didn't notice when a man, apparently an out-of-towner, approached the cashier and asked if a Mr. Berk was on the premises.

He came over, tapped me on the shoulder and asked, "Are you Mr. Berk?" I answered in the affirmative. He sat down next to me, took ten dollars out of his pocket and said, "This ten dollar bill is yours, and I have a story to tell you.

"Most people have forgotten how tough things were during 1939 and 1940. Some of us were still without jobs, living from hand to mouth, often sleeping in hobo jungles and eating hobo stew from a pot full of contributions from the hoboes and bums on hand that evening. I owned nothing but the shabby clothes on my back.

SETTING AN EXAMPLE

"My one hope was the promise I had just received of a job in Marinette, Wisconsin, a mere sixty miles away. It might as well have been on the moon. I had no money for bus fare, and even if I could find a way to get there, I'd never be given the job because of my long, unkempt hair, and my dirty, slightly torn shirt.

"The next morning I walked into this drug store looking for a handout. While I was here, I spoke to the girl at the register and explained my desperate situation. There was a man sitting at the counter who overheard our converstation. He walked up to me and gave me a ten dollar bill. My mouth dropped open in surprise and before I could thank him he was out the door.

"Believe it or not, that ten dollars enabled me to get a haircut, a shower, and a new shirt. And, I had enough left over to take the bus to Marinette, where I got the job.

"That remarkably kind man was your father, and in addition to this ten dollars, I owe him my life."

My father had died while I was in the Army, so he never heard the story of how much good his gift had done. But he didn't help a stranger to gain recognition. Even when things were tough for him, he always gave a hand where needed. The act itself and the inner satisfaction he felt was his reward.

—*Lesson learned*: While we may never know, true acts of kindness live on long after we are gone.

HE'S SAILING ALONG
Lesson learned by William R. Carver

Guests attending the birthday party for Bill Carver had to watch their step lest they trip over cans of varnish or get tangled in anchor lines. The back room of Hopkins Marine Hardware in West Plam Beach, Florida, was decked out in honor of Carver, who was as much a fixture at the store as the paint counter where he had been stationed for twenty-five years. He originally gained his nautical expertise by caring for five boats of his own, and all of Hopkins' regular customers enjoyed hearing his seafaring tales.

Carver has made "a powerful impression" on a lot of people, his boss told Douglas Kalajian of the *Palm Beach Post* during the back room festivities. "Bill's amazing. He knows everything. He keeps track of every item in the store. He doesn't call in sick. Even if he has a doctor's appointment, he comes in right after."

So? It's of special interest to note that Carver was celebrating his ninety-fifth birthday—but he hastened to tell everyone that he had no plans to retire.

"I like to stay active," Carver said, "I keep moving. The doctor says you use it or you lose it. I'm going to keep using it as long as I can."

Mr. Smith Goes Home Again
Bill Bartell

When I was a youngster growing up in Southern
Illinois, one of the town residents was George Smith
(his real name). I remember that he always had time to
spend with us kids—we'd walk down the street with
him and he would tell us fishing and hunting stories
and he would chuckle a lot, and so would we. We
would look for him coming just so we could tag along
with him.

Mr. Smith was getting along in years—I don't really
know how old he was and I don't recall we ever
thought about it, because it didn't matter. Everybody
loved him. He always wore a smile, always said hello to
passersby, and always helped a lady cross the street.

Those were the days in my boyhood when we had
scooters, those wonderful vehicles (forerunners of
today's fancy metal ones) we made for ourselves from
two-by-fours and broken roller skates; when the iceman
delivered ice by the chunk and my folks put a printed
card in the window to tell him what size block to leave;
when Monday night was "Bank Night" at our town's
movie house and the prize might climb as high as
eighty dollars.

Mr. Smith would tell us about even earlier days,

81

when he lived on a farm and carried spring water to the house for drinking and cooking and they used kerosene lamps to read by, and when fires were fought by bucket brigade. He even claimed he saw some real indians one time on a trip to Oklahoma.

He told us that the first car his dad owned only had two cylinders, and how he saw the first-ever biplanes land in a pasture south of town, and how he went to France on a troop ship in the First World War, and all about the big celebration on Armistice Day in 1918. His fish stories were outrageous—but we knew he really did catch some big ones, and set some records, too.

Later I heard people say Mr. Smith was living in the past and, from the way they said it, that was not a good thing to do. I didn't know why it was bad and I never heard an explanation.

The years went by and I often thought of Mr. Smith and particularly those lazy summer days when we walked barefoot with him on the hot concrete sidewalks ("Hot enough to fry a buzzard's egg," he'd say)—not really going anywhere, just walking.

I'm getting on in years myself and quite often discover I'm chuckling when I recall those scooters, and shooting marbles in the dirt, and building soapbox racers and that sort of thing. And today I have a few fish stories of my own to tell. Strangely enough, though, I don't think those thoughts are "bad"—and not everyone is turned off when I slip into some tale about yesterday.

SETTING AN EXAMPLE

Just a few weeks ago I saw a man who looked exactly like Mr. Smith did long ago. It suddenly came to me that Mr. Smith's remembrances weren't signs of living in the past at all. He was simply sharing his memories—sharing precious moments in his life and doing so with enthusiasm. And I realized, too, that I am becoming a Mr. Smith of sorts to a few youngsters (and a handful of oldsters as well). I tell them stories and it's fun and we chuckle a lot as we walk along or lounge under an umbrella.

A famous writer once said that you can't go home again, but now I know that's not true. Mr. Smith went home many times.

—*Lesson learned*: I can go home, and you can, too, if you want. Just give it a try, and if anyone says you're living in the past, say, "Yes, I am, and enjoying it immensely—thanks to Mr. Smith."

FIVE

JUST FOR FUN

A merry heart doeth good like a medicine.
—Proverbs 17:22

Handle with Care
Sid Wallach

It had been twenty-six years since my heart attack and I had convinced myself that I was home free. But, alas—not so. While I was enjoying a pleasant walk on a cold winter day, suddenly an excruciating chest pain almost dropped me to the sidewalk. It had hit unexpectedly, but I knew immediately that my heart-honeymoon had ended. This was big trouble—to the extent that I was not at all sure I could walk the three blocks back to my house. However, I did manage to get there by moving slowly and assuring myself that this episode was only a warning; I might not be able to postpone the bypass surgery which my doctor had cautioned me earlier seemed inevitable.

After consulting with the doctor, I checked into Buffalo General Hospital and began the various preparatory steps prior to the possible bypass operation. In due course I was wheeled down to the prep room, which had four spaces on one side for those patients going in and four spaces on the other side for those coming out. I was visited on the going-in side by a pleasant nurse wearing a surgical mask. She said, "I'm going to prep you for this procedure (an angiogram to specifically pinpoint the heart blockage), but I can't stay in the room with you because I'm pregnant and there is an X-ray machine used in the process."

This procedure requires the making of an incision in

the groin to insert a catheter in the artery leading up into the heart. So, she wheeled me into the room and "prepped" me. And, if you don't know what that means, it involves a razor and the very close shaving of a very private part.

My doctor performed the angiogram and exclaimed with some glee (it seemed to me), "Wallach, you won't get away with it this time! It's a bypass for you. Just look at this mess."

I was then wheeled out to the side for patients coming out and my pregnant nurse came over to me and said, "You are to lie flat on your back and you cannot lift your right leg because we are going to put pressure there to close the incision. However, you had a little high blood pressure so we had to give you some medication which will make you want to pee." *And indeed she was right; the urge hit me as she was speaking.*

To this revelation I replied with a lot of logic, "If I'm flat on my back and cannot move my right leg, how can I pee?"

She said, "I have my own system." *The urge was getting more urgent by the second,* "You lift your left leg until your ankle is up to your hip." *Just hurry, I thought!* "You then place this bottle alongside your thigh," *Ple-e-ease hurry!* "and then you put your . . . Oh, here, let me do it for you!"

I laughed. So did she. And the memory of that scene, even later during the by-pass "event," gave me more than one hearty chuckle.

—*Lesson learned:* If you are going to have an angiogram, get a nice nurse!

Just Send Money
Jim Atkins

As an inquisitive newspaper reporter who moved into his "after fifty" cycle of life several years ago, I often find myself pondering the everyday traditions we have come to accept without question. For example, the mailman, the garbage man, the bartender, the cab driver, the barber, the waitress, all expect tips.

Like almost every other subgroup in the country, waitresses have their own Web page. They call it the Waitressing Gripe Page and they want you to be nicer and tip them more.

In their Web page they gripe about bad tippers and list the most stupid questions customers ask. A recent entry in this department was about a customer who asked what was the difference in size between the eight-inch and the twelve-inch pizza.

Speaking of pizza, the pizza delivery men want to get more dough. So they built their own Web page to get their message out.

The writer of the pizza Web page complains many people just tip one dollar on a twenty-five-dollar pizza order. He argues a pizza delivery man should get better tips than a waitress. Why? Because they are paid minimum wage, have to furnish their car and pay for their gas, risk their lives in traffic, and are targets for criminals because they carry food and money.

Deadpan comic Stephen Wright says some even have to make pies when they are not delivering them. He says he knows this pizza delivery man who works at a pizza restaurant where they only sell slices. When the pizza delivery man is not on deliveries the boss has him twirling triangles of dough in the air.

When I eat in a cafeteria I don't want a waiter to carry my tray to the table for an expected tip. One good reason for eating in a cafeteria is you don't have to tip.

My number-one complaint is those jars you find in self-service restaurants. The jars usually have a sign on them stating, "Tips Appreciated." I'm supposed to get my own coffee and then tip for this non-service?

Nobody's gonna push me around, so I'm planning to start a Web page on the art of tipping.

I also plan to educate people to tip reporters. For example, people who like to read my newspaper column could tip me. If I were tipped I bet I could write those columns a lot faster. Or when I cover a boring town commission meeting, the town could tip me. Or let's say Dan Rather does a good show, why not send him a ten-dollar tip? Or if Matt Drudge writes an item that turns out to be true, I say send him a one-dollar tip.

—*Lesson learned:* I have just learned this is a new way for me to make money. I simply have to work out a system for determining *how much* you should tip reporters.

Logic of the Young

Feliciana O. McClead

Since my retirement at age sixty, ten years ago, I have been able to give more love and attention to my grandchildren. I marveled at the logic of my grandson, Sam, when at age four he promised me a computer as soon as he grew up and made money. At age five he announced that he intended to move into our house after we died because somebody had to guard it.

Approaching his fifth birthday he looked forward to his birthday party. My husband was in and out of hospitals at the time because of heart problems, and Sam invited him to the party if he was "still alive." (He wanted his grandpa to have something to look forward to!)

My husband, who is five-foot-eleven and weighs two hundred pounds, asked Sam, then age seven, if he would push his wheelchair if he ever needed to be in one. Sam said, "No." I then aked him if he would push grandma's wheelchair. I am four-foot-eleven and weigh one hundred pounds. Without hesitation he said he sure would. My husband chastised him for his preferential treatment, but Sam gave us a very sensible and logical reply. He said, "But Grandpa, I can see over Grandma's head."

—*Lesson learned*: It's true. Out of the mouths of babes (sometimes!) comes wisdom.

Many Mini-Lessons

I've learned not to run for the bus; it leaves faster than it used to.

It seems to me they are making steps higher than in the old days, and have you noticed the smaller print they use in the newspapers?

I've learned that some days you're the dog; some days you're the hydrant.

I've learned it's hard to make a comeback when you haven't been anywhere.

I've learned my joints are more accurate than the National Weather Service.

I've learned that if you walk with your head held high it helps you adjust to your new bifocals.

I've learned that you can tell a lot about people by the way they handle three things: a rainy day, lost luggage, and tangled Christmas tree lights.

JUST FOR FUN

I've learned that *the only time the world beats a path to your door* is when you're in the bathroom.

I've learned that *most of us seniors burn the midnight oil* after 9:00 P.M.

I've learned *a bargain is something you can't use* at a price you can't resist.

I've learned that *exercise is that awful feeling* that will go away if you just lie down for awhile.

Surprise!

Dolores A. Dietz

My husband, Joe, and I were married for forty-five years, and it wasn't easy to think of what to buy each other for Christmas. And here we were at that time of year again.

For myself, I decided I wanted a small battery-operated television set to take outside in the summer and to use when we had a power outage. I started looking at TV's while I was shopping for a gift for Joe, and I found just the set I wanted. I decided to buy it and save my husband a trip to the store to buy it for me. Besides, it was the last day of the sale.

Joe had gone into the city that day, and on the way home he stopped at his favorite hobby shop. They had a model train engine that would be perfect for his collection. He was going to tell me about it and hope I would be able to buy it for him for Christmas. But, then he decided to buy it and save me the trip. Besides, it was the last one.

I arrived home and pulled into the driveway just as Joe got there and drove right in behind me. He got out of the car and was all excited. He said, "Wait 'til you see what I bought for you to give me for Christmas." And I said, "Wait 'til you see what I bought for you to give me."

Then I figured, "Wait a minute. Don't tell me, and I won't tell you. You wrap your gift and I'll wrap mine. On Christmas day you will be surprised at what I get, and I will be surprised at what you get!"

We both were surprised and happy with our gifts on Christmas morning. It was a great way to start the day!

—*Lesson learned*: Don't be afraid to use your imagination to make excitement out of the routine.

Where's the Restroom?

Virginia Brodin

My husband is a sea captain and thanks to his position I have traveled extensively with him around the globe. Naturally, I have had occasion in various countries to inquire about where I might find a restroom. I learned long ago that such rooms are identified by many different names and come in a wide variety of shapes and forms.

Some time back I discovered a great, informative book called I *Hear America Talking* by Stuart Berg Flexner. Mr. Flexner has devoted a section to tracing, along with other vital facts, the first use of the word *restroom*. It goes back to about 1900. Further, he tells us that such rooms were called "public comfort stations" after 1904.

On my first visit to England, I found the British call it the "W.C.," for *water closet*, a term Mr. Flexner traces back to the 1750s. (Leave it to the Brits to hang on to tradition.) Would I get help if I asked for the W.C. in China? I doubt it.

When I was growing up, the popular name I used was "powder room." Hence, I was quite fascinated to learn that back in the 1920s, if I were a speakeasy patron, I would be directed to the ladies' "powder room," which then may have come from the colonial "powder room" where men withdrew to powder their wigs. Mr. Flexner tells us that perhaps "it may have come into use in the 1920s simply because now for the first time many women were using or admitting to using powder."

In my travels, a problem I had that was bigger than finding a restroom in the first place was how to flush the darned things once you're there. In Morocco many were only places for your feet and a hole in the floor. No flusher! In India there was a button on the floor to step on. Spain had a knob in the top of the tank either to push or pull. It seemed every country had a different system. Sometimes I left the "John" in frustration, not being able to find any flushing device.

By the way, the word "John," Mr. Flexner advises, was used early on by men to refer to the privy. "Jake" had meant a privy in England since 1530, and John was in use by the 1650s. The word *bathroom* became a generally known term in the 1830s—and it was just that: a room for taking a bath.

I got a surprise during a restroom visit at a golf club in England. My husband and I were having lunch with some friends and after a round of cocktails the need arose for me to find the "room." No problem with the language. My hostess said, "It's just up the steps; first door on the right."

When I arrived in the "stall," I noticed a rather heavy chain hanging from the ceiling near a large white tank. Aha! The W.C. and its flusher! Upon leaving the room I pulled the chain—and the lights went out!

So much for my expertise in finding flushers.

—*Lesson learned:* When in Rome, do as the Romans do. Anyplace else, you're on your own.

SECRETS REVEALED!

Mel Brooks, "The 2,000-Year-Old Man," in an interview with Claudia Dreifus for *Modern Maturity*, offered some secrets he had learned which promote long life:

"Never touch fried foods. Eat plenty of garlic so the angel of death won't kiss you. Pounds of garlic. Eat lightly. Many, many berries. Very good, very anti-cancer, these berries. And never retire! Do what you do and keep doing it. But don't do it on Friday. Take Friday off. Friday, Saturday, and Sunday do fishing, do sexual activities, watch Fred Astaire movies. Then from Monday to Thursday do what you've been doing all your life, unless it's lifting bags of potatoes off the back of a truck. I mean, after eighty-five that's hard to do."

How to Bathe a Cat

Fifty-plussers have learned a lesson from veterinarian Jeffrey LaCroix: how to handle the tricky job of bathing a cat. He passes along these instructions from an unknown author.

Cat bathing is a martial art:

1. Know that although the cat has the advantage of quickness and lack of concern for human life, you have the advantage of strength. Capitalize on that advantage by selecting the battlegroud. Pick a very small bathroom.

   If your bathroom is more than four feet square, I recommend that you get in the tub with the cat and close the sliding glass doors. (A simple shower curtain will not do. A berserk cat can shred a three-ply rubber shower curtain in a matter of seconds.)

2. Know that a cat has claws and will not hesitate to remove all the skin from your body. Your advantge here is that you are smart and know how to dress to protect yourself. I recommend canvas overalls tucked into high-top construction boots, a pair of steel-mesh gloves, an army helmet, a hockey face-mask, and a long-sleeve flak jacket.

3. Pick up your cat nonchalantly, as if to carry him to his supper dish. (Cats will not usually notice your strange attire.)

4. In a single liquid motion, shut the bathroom door, step into the tub enclosure, slide the glass door shut, dip the cat in the water and squirt him with shampoo. You have begun one of the wildest forty-five seconds of your life.

5. Cats have no handles. Add the fact that he now has soapy fur, and the problem is radically compounded. Do not expect to hold on to him for more than two or three seconds at a time. When you have him, however, you must remember to give him another squirt of shampoo and rub like crazy. He'll then spring free and fall back into the water, thereby rinsing himself off.

6. Next, the cat must be dried. This is simple compared with what you have just been through. That's because by now the cat is semi-permanently affixed to your right leg. You simply pop the drain plug with your foot, reach for your towel and wait.

   After all the water is drained from the tub, it is a simple matter to reach down and dry the cat.

In a few days the cat will relax enough to be removed from your leg. He will usually have nothing to say for about three weeks and will spend a lot of time sitting with his back to you.

You will be tempted to assume he is angry. This usually isn't the case. As a rule he is simply plotting ways to get through your defenses and injure you for life the next time you decide to give him a bath.

But at least now he smells a lot better.

PEOPLE ARE YOUNGER THAN THEY USED TO BE

Author Unknown (submitted by Marjorie Free)

I have learned that everything is farther away now than it used to be. It is twice as far to the corner and they have added a hill, I've noticed.

There is no sense in asking anyone to read aloud. Everyone speaks in such a low voice that I can hardly hear them. The material in clothes is getting so skimpy . . . especially around the waist and hips.

Even people are changing; they are so much younger than they used to be when I was their age. On the other hand, people my own age are so much older than I am. I ran into an old friend the other day, and she had changed so much she didn't recognize me.

I got to thinking about the poor thing while I was combing my hair this morning, and in doing so I glanced at my reflection. They don't even make good mirrors like they used to!

My Dream

Last night I dreamed
I was young again.
And my feet didn't hurt
And my knees would still bend.

There were no sagging wrinkles
No lines 'round my mouth
And I noticed my fanny
Had not yet gone south.

I danced in my dream
And I did foolish things
My heart was on fire
And my body had wings.

And then I woke up
And was happy to see
That I was still old
And I was still me.

I've learned lots of lessons
I didn't know then
So I'd rather be wiser
Than younger again!

—Jean Moyer

SIX

POSITIVE OUTLOOK

To look up and not down,
To look forward and not back,
To look out and not in, and
To lend a hand.
—Edward Everett Hale

The Accidental Writer

Shirley Barksdale

The year I turned fifty-two, life dealt me a series of blows that made me a candidate for a straightjacket. In less than nine months, my mother died and then my son died. Then, after twenty-five years in Colorado, my husband was transferred to California.

I did not adapt easily to the fast lane of the Golden State. I longed for my home and my friends, and I wanted to stop crying. So in desperation I braved the terrifying freeways and headed for Adult Education—not for enlightenment, but for companionship. At admissions I was told that the Spanish class I sought was already filled; however, an upholstery class and a creative writing class were still open.

I opted for creative writing, even though it was only slightly more tempting than upholstery. But I'd walked blocks from my parking space and was soaked to the bone in a downpour. I needed a place, any place, to dry out. I slipped behind the last vacant desk and listened to serious students declare their lofty writing goals. Before I could bolt for the door, it came my turn to speak up. Cotton-mouthed, I wailed, "I'm new here and I'm homesick and I'm soaking wet and I'm in the wrong class. . . ."

The instructor, a fiery redheaded drill sergeant, recognized hysteria when she heard it. "Enough," she barked, "just write it up for next week's assignment." No way, I thought, will I return to this writing thing.

But loneliness triggers bizarre behavior, and I did return. Not daring to face the instructor empty-handed, I plucked away on the old portable typewriter. Creating, spilling my guts. Three hours before class, I reread my manuscript and realized in shame that I had written a 1,500-word litany of anger, grief, and self-pity. Frantically I rewrote; this time I changed the tone from gloom to humor, poking fun at myself.

I did not expect to hear my effort read aloud in the instructor's determined voice. Now sweat—not rain—dripped off my brow. But miracle of miracles, the class applauded at the end. Someone gave me a title, another a possible market, and still another showed me how to prepare it for submission.

Their advice paid off. Before the next meeting, I had a seventy-five-dollar check from the *San Jose Mercury News* and a note from the editor complimenting the article. The only person more shocked than I was the instructor who had literally scared me into writing.

Once hooked, I stayed with my slave driver through three semesters. Although writing did not totally assuage my grief, it rescued me from the brink of self-destruction. Today, because of a series of improbable events that sent me to a creative writing class instead of Spanish 101,

POSITIVE OUTLOOK

I have made wonderful new friends, I have come to love our adopted state of California, and over the years I have enjoyed the thrill of seeing my byline in major publications.

—*Lesson learned*: The mature years should never be a deterrent to expanding one's horizons, and life does not end because of aging or overwhelming grief.

Make Time to Fulfill Dreams
Dorothy Girling

One day I was in the kitchen working, sweat on my brow, standing amidst a clutter of heavy pots and pans. Impulsively I stopped to question myself. Here I was at age fifty-two, a school cook preparing meals for seven hundred children each day, starting at 7:00 A.M. and working straight through until 2:00 P.M. The disturbing question unexpectedly had popped into my mind. "Here I am working myself to death day in and day out. When will I ever have time to fulfill my lifelong dreams of painting and becoming an artist?"

As I needed to continue my cooking job for financial reasons, the luxury of not working was not an option. I decided at that critical moment I could no longer use lack of time as an excuse. I would simply make time.

That day after work I went home and took a nap, fixed supper and ate, then got out my painting materials and began painting. With a totally new determination I painted until midnight. I arose the next morning fresh and ready to go back to work. The prospect of overcoming the time barrier made me feel like an entirely different person.

I actually spent some of my hard-earned money on myself and enrolled in an art workshop. After a few classes I was encouraged by my instructor to enter local art shows, which I did. I was accepted by some but not all—just enough to keep the fire burning within me.

Now that I am over seventy-five, I look back at the wonderful life I began to build twenty-four years earlier by "creating" time for myself. After I retired as the school cook, I was well along in my art career and my adventurous life began. I have been in hundreds of art shows, both indoors and on outdoor sidewalks and streets. I overcame my shyness and gave some talks to women's groups; I still demonstrate painting techniques each year at the county fair; I volunteer to sketch kids at the annual women's club festival; I taught watercoloring to kindergarten children, and volunteered just over a year ago to teach seniors at our senior center.

I am happy that I have been able to show someone how to do something, then to observe the pleasure they get from their accomplishment—which is all the payment I need. The kindergarten children loved the miracle of color changes as colors ran together. To them everything was a "miracle." When I sketch the older children at the festival, it's pleasing to watch the mothers and their reaction to their youngsters' "portraits."

Most of all, it is especially rewarding to work with the seniors. Like myself, most of them put off things they wanted while they worked and raised their families. Now some of them also have found a whole new world and new friends.

—*Lesson learned:* Volunteering has its rewards. I am much happier since I made the time to give happiness.

Listen! I'm Playing My Song
Katherine Runyan

Most folks have to turn on their car radio if they want to listen to music while they drive. Not me. I'm surrounded by music all the time—almost too much—driving or not. You see, I have tinnitus.

Maybe you have heard of this thing, and maybe not. It's an impairment that sometimes comes with hearing loss. I have a rhythmic ringing and roaring inside my head that causes me to hear music I had memorized over the years. Because I have been a popular music fan all my life, I have a vast store of golden oldies to draw from. Occasionally I break out in a vocal sing-along, usually unaware that I am doing so. It's sometimes awkward. I once sang out, "Be My Love" to a horrified/ flattered stranger I didn't realize was there. Once I told my husband he was, "A worrisome thing who'll leave you to sing the blues in the night."

I have hearing aids, amplified home devices, and a remarkably understanding husband who yells sweet nothings in my ear. Still, the beat goes on!

Actually, I'm not as bad off as a friend who was convinced everyone could hear the same cacophony she did and wondered why the librarian allowed all that noise. One day, before I retired, I was toting "that barge" and lifting "that bale" while typing data into the computer and heard my supervisor mutter, "Where does she get those songs?" So, from then on at work, instead of rolling along with "Old Man River," I immediately entered still waters and kept my mouth shut. However, dredging up old songs gave us plenty of trivia fun at breaks and lunch. I think I'm the only one who remembered the Maharajah song:

> There's a rich Maharajah of Magador
> Who had ten thousand camels and maybe more.
> He had rubies and pearls
> And the loveliest girls,
> But he didn't know how to do
> The rumba.

I did recall all the words: the Maharajah gave up everything but his harem, and got his rumba lessons. Okay, so it isn't great culture, but it's fun. And it's sort of a celebration of my hearing days when I was able to listen and learn all of the popular songs of the time.

So, if I can learn to harness my tinnitus to my advantage, I'll have the world at my ears. Why, I could even practice an entire oratorio before Christmas!

—*Lesson learned:* Make lemonade from life's lemons, and remember that the hardiest flavor is from zest!

LEARN FROM THIS MAN? YOU BET!

Fred W. Hooper, one of the giants of horse racing, was born on a farm in Georgia. He quit school in the eighth grade, he raised cotton, he broke horses, he even went to barber school and cut hair for a living. He worked as a school teacher, a carpenter, a riveter, a prizefighter by night and a potato farmer by day. And after a blight ruined his potato crop, he borrowed money to get a job building a road, and became rich.

He formed the Hooper Construction Company and became one of the major contractors in the Southeast.

In 1943, for ten thousand dollars, he bought a colt which he named Hoop, Jr., after his son, Fred, Jr. In 1945, Hoop, Jr., ridden by Eddie Arcaro, outran fifteen colts to win the Kentucky Derby. Later, his favorite filly, Susan's Girl, won a total of $1.2 million in purses. In the 1980s another colt of Hooper's, Precisionist, earned more than $3.4 million.

In Hooper's later years he was somewhat limited in his ability to walk, but he moved about with the aid of a cane or a walker or, when he visited racetracks, a wheelchair.

At the age of 101, he was still able to walk with a walker to his box at Gulfstream racetrack in Florida.

His wife, Wanda, remembered that he had once suffered a broken neck in a car crash but survived after nine months in the hospital. She also remembered that he played excellent golf into his eighties despite many other injuries. "He's like a cat," she said. "He's got nine lives, and always planning."

When he was asked how a man who had lived a century explains it, he responded with his lesson learned: "Hard work. And always look ahead. Don't look back."

Fred Hooper died in 2000 at the age of 102.

—W.B.T.

Natalie's Gift
Lee Berk

My wife, Natalie, was one of those rare persons with a ready wit and a warm personality instantly apparent to everyone she met. She was a philosopher of sorts and a collector of words of wisdom from newspapers and newsletters. She clipped them like some women clip recipes and tucked them away in various places for safe-keeping. But she didn't just file them, she collected the wisdom in her head and heart and lived by their positive philosophy. I always marveled at her even disposition and how we managed to disagree agreeably!

In our many years of marriage, I never heard her say anything unpleasant about another human being (even though I'm sure she was tempted more than once during her tenure as a condominium president).

Our mornings together were delightful as we amused one another with tidbits from the paper. She always laughed enthusiastically at my attempts at humor and obvious puns, and while I would be working at deciphering jumbled quotes and quips of the day, she would start solving the crossword puzzle. I still feel her presence in the mornings as I struggle with my word games and I sometimes speak out loud to her.

Shortly after she passed away, I noticed for the first

time a clipping she had taped to the inside of her medicine cabinet. I didn't know it then but it was the Optimist's creed. I read it with tears in my eyes as I saw Natalie in every word.

I read the first sentence: "Be so strong that nothing can disturb your mind." That's her, I said to myself as I recalled the many examples of her strength in the face of crisis. My son Jeff (by a previous marriage) was hit by a speeding car as he crouched with another young man over an injured dog in the street. He was left with shattered thigh bones and it was Natalie who was our hero through the difficult two years of recuperation.

The next sentence was "Talk health, happiness, and prosperity to everyone you meet." I recall how she propped us up when there was little hope of Jeff ever being able to walk again. We badly needed encouragement. Thank God, his recovery has been almost complete except for an awkward gait. Natalie helped give him the will to continue his uphill battle along the entire way.

"Make all your friends feel that there is something special in them. Look at the sunny side of everything. Think only the best, work only for the best, and expect only the best. Be as enthusiastic about the success of others as you are about your own." I see Natalie in every word and understand how she was able to gather so many dear and close friends wherever she lived.

"Forget the mistakes of the past and press on to

greater achievements of the future. Give everyone a smile. Spend so much time improving yourself that you have no time left to criticize others. Be too big for worry and too noble for anger."

I sat in my soft leather recliner with that much-read clipping in my hand. I saw Natalie in her familiar place beside me and I marveled at her ability to put those simple words into a way of life. I have wondered many times since finding that clipping taped to her cabinet door if she knew I would discover it and pass it along to our children and to others.

—*Lesson learned*: A good life and good deeds do not die. They continue to inspire us by their example.

What Do You Want?

Stephen Press

When I was accepted into the New York University Theater Department I was seventeen years old. The last question that was asked of me at my acceptance interview was, "What do you want from the theatre?"

My answer was, "When I'm sixty-five years old, I want to say that I've earned my living in the theater." I was seventeen years old when I said that. At seventeen, being sixty-five seemed a long way away and very old.

I turned sixty-five recently and I thought about that answer. First of all, I now think that sixty-five is not old at all! But how have I done with my life plan?

Within three months after graduating from New York University I was on Broadway in *The Diary of Anne Frank*. From then on I never did anything but theater to pay my bills. I've taught theater, acted, directed, wrote, and produced. I am a member of Actors' Equity Association, the Screen Actors Guild, the American Federation of Television and Radio Artists, the Dramatists Guild, and the Society of Stage Directors and Choreographers. Theater has been my life and it has been wonderful.

A play that I wrote, *The Last Carnival*, was just published by Samuel French, Inc., the largest play publisher in the world. I also directed a production of *The Last Carnival* this past summer. Just before that I acted in a new film. A year ago I directed a production of William Shakespeare's *A Midsummer Night's Dream*, and before that I directed . . . but you get the picture.

Along with my career, my wife and I have raised two children. One is a doctor in New York City and the other makes her living as an art director at a large Madison Avenue advertising agency.

Now that I have reached my first career goal, it's time to set a new one: I want to continue working in the theatre for the next fifty years. Call me in 2051 to see how I'm doing, and if you happen to be casting a good role or need an experienced director or need a playwright, I'm sure I'll be able to accomodate you!

—*Lesson learned:* I've learned that the key to success is to find the thing you love to do. If you do it well, keep at it all your life. It's a can't-fail prescription for happiness.

Those Golden Years?

Phyllis G. Tritsch

One day recently, after planting a few flowers in the garden, I found myself exhausted. Earlier, I had discovered that hopping up off the floor was a thing of the past. And who was this person who suddenly needed to lie down in the middle of the day? I became frustrated that I couldn't do all the physical things I had done before. I thought, "Golden Years? Phooey! Whoever thought up that description of aging must have been twenty years old."

But since then, I have changed my mind. There are indeed golden moments to savor and enjoy. Instead of bewailing the things I can no longer do, I have chosen to list all the things I *can* do that light up my life.

There is the golden moment when I get a telephone call from a grandchild to tell me of some small success at school or at work. Or the golden moment of sitting on the porch, overlooking a wildlife preserve and watching the sun set in a blaze of colors and reminding me of how wonderful it is to be there to enjoy it.

There is the golden moment when my spouse of all those many years says, "Hey, you look beautiful!" and plants a kiss on my lips. There are countless golden moments in e-mails and letters from old friends who want to keep in touch and share their lives with me. It is truly a golden moment at the bridge table to play a good hand and make that impossible bid and hear my partner say, "Well played!"

That energetic bluejay who cavorts in the bird bath flapping his wings and making the water fly in every direction is a golden moment to be enjoyed over and over again.

So, you see, life is full of Golden Moments. We just have to be on the lookout every day in order to recognize them. For us, those things are no longer the background of life, they are the essence of it.

—*Lesson learned*: The wonderful part of aging is that we have the time and the good sense to savor and enjoy the special times. And, yes, these *are* the "Golden Years!"

Finding a New Direction

Lori Selby-Dailey

The day my husband was airlifted to the hospital he had played twenty-seven holes of golf, and he smiled at me as they were putting him aboard the helicopter. He died within hours and I had lost my first love and best friend.

Ours was a fairy-tale marriage of thirty-two years. He was gentle, considerate and affectionate, and until that dream-shattering day I would still get butterflies when he walked unexpectedly into the room.

I was sure my life was over when he died. I struggled through the horror of all the death arrangements by resolving in my heart to join him soon (by way of sleeping pills) when everything was settled. I didn't think about how my suicide would affect our sons, or how hurt family and friends would be. My sole concern was to end the agony of loss that I carried constantly. I was sure the pain I was enduring was uniquely mine.

Luckily, a few good friends sensed my plan and insisted that I join a bereavement therapy group. I resisted, but because of their persistent prodding I soon agreed just to keep them quiet.

In that special group, I met a young lady who had lost her husband suddenly, the same way I did. The big difference, however, was that she had two babies to bring up without a father. In my case, my three sons were grown and had the privilege and pleasure of having had a loving father to help mold their future.

I held an older woman who watched her husband suffer for four long, painful years before death set him free. Her last memories were of an old and bitterly angry man. By contrast, my husband managed a smile even at the end.

I comforted a young woman who lost her mom—her last living relative. Now all her family was gone. I still had a mother and father and children to comfort me.

Our counselor let us cry, encouraged us to talk, and insisted we hug each other. The caring came naturally.

It's so hard to feel sorry for yourself when there are others around you suffering just as much if not more. It doesn't negate your loss, but in the act of comforting another, you find comfort for yourself. And when you feel sorrow for someone else's pain, it's hard to wallow in your own misery.

I feel I helped these special friends, and I know they helped me. For quite a while afterwards we would meet socially. Occasionally we would cry together, but mostly we'd laugh and have fun, and we still send cards to one another. I thank them sincerely. They saved my life.

—*Lesson learned:* I look ahead now and not back. I thank God every day that I was given the strength and good sense to see past my problems and into the hearts of others. I learned we must give help in order to receive it.

Acceptance
Jane Ritter

My two children, Stephen and Renee, never knew their father. He was an American jet pilot shot down over Korea more than fifty years ago.

They were too young at the time to have any lasting rememberances of him. Sadly, we never learned what happened to him—a nagging and depressing void that has required blind acceptance over the span of five decades.

Several months ago, at age seventy-five, I suffered a paralyzing stroke. I can still function, but in limited ways. I am not able to stand, much less walk. I am unable to do anything requiring two hands, like needle-work, which could relieve boredom. Nonetheless, I can still write, and my current project is in response to my children wanting to know more about their father and relatives they never knew. So I am writing stories going back to the Civil War, when my grandparents were born.

From all this I have learned acceptance—not necessarily an easy feat. It is challenging, indeed, having to accept help with the simplest things mixed with having gratitude for the smallest everyday gift in living. I have graciously accepted living in a nursing home, where now most of my new friends are in wheelchairs.

It tests anyone's sense of humor. Still, there are things to laugh about, like the time a gentleman in a wheelchair said he wanted me to be his girlfriend. This man had four warts clustered on his forehead and assured me he wouldn't "bother me a lot, maybe just once or twice a year." Humor is around us; it just takes a little longer to recognize it.

Many years ago I learned the consequences of resistance: the more I resisted change, the more barriers seemed to keep me in the same place—there was no change; no progress for me. Any movement forward came after I stopped resisting. I took a reality check. Magically, things changed for the better. That's not to say that I didn't do my share toward improvement.

When I think of what I used to take for granted, like driving any place I wanted to, I quickly put that thought aside and toodle around in my mechanical wheelchair (without a helmet), riding both outdoors and inside my new home where we are addressed as residents, not patients, and learn to accept our new life.

I am grateful, however, that I can see and hear and talk, but with the stroke my singing voice is gone completely. I, who used to sing Mozart and Puccini, can't even hum now. Oh well, at least I did it at one time. Today is a different time in a different place.

A young friend recently said, "Jane, you've worked all your life; look at this situation as time off. No cleaning, no cooking, no laundry. You can rest when you want to; have your meals on a tray in bed. Not all bad!"

I do listen to such words of comfort—but then try to lose myself remembering my children's father and writing about him.

—*Lesson learned*: In addition to acceptance, I have learned to have patience with myself and with those caring for me.

Thank My Son
Marian Brovero

When Ray, our oldest of three sons, lost his hard-fought battle with cancer, he was not quite twenty-four and I was forty-seven. Years of my life had been filled with a mother's dreams and proud expectations of the kind of man he would become. But the future had abruptly ended.

At first, his loss brought pain and sorrow too deep and too lasting for me to share or explain to anyone. It was my burden alone and I felt my very soul had been crushed. In those dark hours I longed for just a brief rest from my distress, or at least some much-needed assistance in coping with it. But I failed to find either.

Ray was a constant source of inspiration to others and a gold medal winner for bravery. To the very end, those close to him could see his courage as well as his consideration and kind spirit shining through his struggle.

It took me ten years, until I was in my late fifties, to once again laugh a deep belly laugh or to cry at sad endings of movies—I had already cried too much. Life without Ray's loving presence had continued to sap energy from me even after I thought there was none left to give.

I finally realized that even though total recovery

might not be possible, serious self-evaluation was the surest way for me to improve my life. By turning my thoughts inward, I soon learned that I had much time to make up for my decade of depression. How many opportunities had I missed to enjoy my other two sons and their children as they were growing? Why hadn't I been running to offer comfort to others who were also suffering? I was too occupied with my own personal loss.

Caring and compassion have now become the code by which I survive without Ray, and they permit me to be a benefactor to my other sons and the people whose lives I touch.

Much of my time is spent writing—which is a helpful therapy often recommended by psychologists, who call it "expressive" or "confessional" writing. The benefits of writing about traumatic experiences, they say, can go beyond the soothing of the mind to actually mending the body. One psychology professor at the University of Texas declares that "being able to put [upsetting] experiences into words is good for your physical health." Earlier, much of my writing was about my loss of Ray, but now I write advice articles for grandparents as well as the young parents in today's difficult world. When a publisher says "No," I merely write a friend and include my thoughts in the letter.

Today I see young Ray in the words and ways of his brothers. And his thirst for knowledge appears to have found a home in five grandchildren he would have laughed with and pitched a mean baseball to. My heart is lighter because I see him around me in many ways, whether I am comforting a recent widow or babysitting for a new mother. It was Ray who taught me caring and compassion—and when those I am helping thank me, I simply say, "You can thank my son."

—*Lesson learned*: Don't let grieving consume your life. Take comfort in paying tribute to your loved one by sharing his or her love with others.

SEVEN

FAMILY TIES

Common blood is a bond to be cherished
and nurtured forever.

—*Anonymous*

Love Comes in All Sizes
Bard Lindeman

For the past eighteen years, I have written a syndicated newspaper column for the Chicago Tribune group. Six years ago I began sponsoring a contest for grandparents. I challenged my readers to send me a favorite story about a grandchild.

Jack Jacobson, then seventy-seven, set up his anecdote by first explaining that for thirty years he and five friends, most of whom work together, have met regularly in hometown Tuscon, Arizona, for coffee and talk. Stories about grandkids and their exploits are standard fare at these gabfests.

When Jacobson's narrative opens, he is driving idly along while next to him is grandson Brent, his "kind, intelligent, thoughtful, fun-to-be-with grandson," just six years old. As the pair ride along, it becomes obvious Brent is thinking. For once, he stays completely silent.

"Usually, he is singing, laughing, joking," says Grandpa Jack, wondering why "my little guy is sitting quietly, hands clasped in his lap." The grandfather inquires: "You okay, Brent?"

The boy nods yes, but then asks: "Grandpa Jack, what did you do before you had me when the guys [your friends] told grandkid stories?"

Grandpa Jack has his answer ready: "Well, Brent, I sat and listened and prayed to myself that one day I'd have a wonderful grandson just like you. Then I would have grandkid stories to tell, too."

The boy continues to sit quitely, still deep in thought.

"You know, Grandpa Jack," he says next, "when I was growing in Mama's belly, I prayed that I would have a wonderful grandpa, just like you."

Again the boy falls silent before adding: "And . . . I got him."

Jack Jacobson writes, "I had to slow the car down just then, for suddenly it became difficult for me to see clearly. . . ."

Many letters from readers speak, in heartfelt language, of what a grandchild means in the life of an often troubled, or depressed, older adult. Of particular poignancy are letters describing a struggle against disease. Carol Feller, of Grayslake, Illinois, writes: "You asked about a grandson's love and understanding. Well, grandson Taigart is the reason I believe I've survived cancer. He never scolded me for not being able to climb trees or ride bikes. He didn't make me feel guilty for not having the energy to bake cookies, or throw him a fastball. He accepted my limitations.

"Once, he asked: 'Boys don't get breast cancer, do they?' Later, with the logic of the child, he said, 'Granny, you won't hurt if you throw the ball with your other arm, will you?' Another suggestion was: 'Take a nap now; then we can go to the park!'

"Yes, my caring grandson showed me how to turn off my fear, to replace it with grudging acceptance. Quite simply, when I am with him, Taigart makes my heart smile."

—Lesson learned: These are our grandchildren, life's bonus. Grandchildren, bless them every one, have turned life around for all of us in the great Gray Legion, and taken the verb love to another level. And, like some magic tonic, they've shown us why we must go on, and endure.

Keep the Legacy Alive
Deborah R. Sackel

By the time I was ten years old, I had lost most of my family, including both of my parents. I was raised by my elderly grandmother and, for whatever reasons, we did not get along. As a rebellious teenager, I had no interest in my heritage or family history.

When I was twenty-one, our home caught fire, taking my grandmother's life. The day after the tragedy (with a backhoe waiting in the background to forever seal the first twenty-one years of my life), I hurriedly sifted through the blackened debris. The whole house had burned and it was apparent that nothing could be salvaged.

Ignoring obvious hazards, something drove me to keep searching. I came upon some charred and soaking-wet boxes buried deep in the back of the cellar. A quick look revealed they contained very old letters and pictures not recognizable to me. However, I took them, and over the next few days I spread the burned, wet contents over the three small rooms of my apartment. When they dried, I repacked them and put them in my storage space without so much as a glance.

Over the past thirty years, my life has taken many twists and turns. I retired recently from a fast-paced, stressful job that required me to work long hours. At last I had time to catch up on those cleaning chores I had put off far too long. It was then, in my cluttered storage area, that I again came across those boxes labeled "1969." I had completely wiped them from my mind, but now I began sorting through them with excitement.

I was amazed at how close the contents had come to complete destruction. Everything was singed around the edges, but for some reason (the efforts of the fire department? or of a higher Power?), they stayed intact.

There were love letters from my grandfather, and a diary my grandmother kept during her pregnancy with my mom. I found negatives that were partly burned, but I took them to a photo specialist anyway. Surprisingly, the blackened negatives produced good prints from the 1920s and 1930s. I saw my grandparents, my great grandmother, my very young mother, and our family estate, named Harbor Hill, in Cold Spring, New York. When my grandfather became ill, my grandmother opened the home as a bed and breakfast, which became a popular place for celebrities to visit and relax in complete privacy. I recalled that as a child I served actress Rita Hayworth and singer Dick Haymes breakfast in bed. Among the salvaged items were scrapbooks with comments from famous people.

To imagine my appreciation of these treasures, think of being an orphan with no records, no family pictures or any documentation of the early decades of your life.

FAMILY TIES

To this day, I am still enjoying the memorabilia, which covers two World Wars and the Depression, and includes countless fascinating stories. I consider myself very lucky to have somehow been given the chance and the good sense to save the boxes from 1969.

—*Lesson learned*: Take the time and interest to learn your family's history, and to protect family treasures. I was retired before I learned this lesson. It was almost too late.

Just Say It
Phyllis G. Tritsch

My husband and I were en route from Florida to
Toronto, Canada, to celebrate our wedding anniversary.
On the spur of the moment we decided to stop off in
New England and surpise our son, Geof, on his fiftieth
birthday.

We called his wife, who thought it was a wonderful
idea and conspired with us to keep it a secret. We
arrived in the late afternoon, while he was at work, and
"hid" the car in a neighbor's driveway so he wouldn't
see it. It all worked perfectly and he was delightfully
surprised. We settled in for a weekend visit.

The following afternoon my daughter-in-law and I
were running some errands when she spoke up.
"Mother," she said, "there is something I would like to
discuss with you, but I'm not sure just how to say it." I
couldn't imagine what made her feel so shy or unsure
of herself. Since we had such a wonderful relationship, I
urged her, "Just say it."

She went on. "Mother, have you ever told Geof how
proud you are of him?" In some confusion I replied,
"But he knows!" to which his wife asked, "But have you
ever told him?"

We discussed it and I realized how right she was.

Actually, I never had said the words. My husband and I are very proud of our son who has established a very successful business of his own, takes wonderful care of his family, and is a warm and loving husband and father. We are so proud of what he has accomplished on his own and by himself. While we have often discussed business decisions with him, congratulated him on successes, given lots of hugs, the truth is we had never said the simple words, "I'm proud of you."

The next evening after dinner, Geof opened all his birthday gifts with his two young sons looking on, so proud of the gifts they had bought with their own money. The last gift he opened was my gift to him. It was a needlepoint project I had worked on for two years: a counted cross-stitch map of the world as it would have looked in 1500. Since the name of his business is "Compass Consulting," the map was framed and intended to decorate his office wall.

He looked at it in amazement, marvelling at the tiny stitches and the intricacy of it, and thanked me with a big hug and tears in his eyes.

This was my opportunity to finally tell him what I had never told him before. "Every stitch," I said, "is my way of telling you how proud your father and I are of you."

His bear hug and tears said it all, but he added, "Mom, I can't tell you how long I have waited to hear you say those words!"

Our two teenaged grandsons looked on with tears in their eyes. I hope they learned the two lessons it had taken me almost seventy-five years to learn.

—*Lesson learned:* Just telling loved ones that you love them isn't enough. They also need to hear that you are proud of them. Don't assume they know. Perhaps they do, but it isn't the same as actually hearing the words from the people who mean the most to them. And, lesson number two, it is never too late to say it.

Reflections on an Empty Nest
Sharon Gagne

Now that my children are grown, I have time for reflection. I have been thinking about the parents, mothers particularly, of previous generations. How different life was for them, and yet so many things seem to remain the same.

I am now at a point in my life when the term "empty nest" applies. I remember hearing that this is a time when many women become depressed because they are faced with something of a mid-life crisis.

My nest is empty, and, to my amazement, I like it! Twenty-eight years of parenting is a long time. Having time to myself to read or for gardening, and simply having freedom of movement is a new-found blessing. I don't miss the soccer practices, or dancing lessons, or sleepovers. However, I am grateful to have experienced those wonderful times.

Perhaps in years past the empty nest was a time for depression and emptiness. However, I can imagine the sheer volume of hard work done in bygone days by mothers with large families and no modern machinery to lighten the load. I can only speculate that they may have been happier than us to see their children head off on their own.

I remember hearing as a little girl that my great-grandmother was a crabby woman. I recall hearing snippets of conversations about her lugging coal for the fire, lopping the heads off chickens for dinner, doing the laundry for a family of ten on a washboard in all kinds of weather. Thinking back, how could she not have been crabby? What a schedule to face! Did she ever have time to read a book? Did she even know how to read? Did she ever take time for herself?

That generation of women couldn't shout about how happy they were to be finished raising a family, because it wouldn't have been proper. (Or maybe they were just too exhausted to let out more than a sigh!)

Today, experts are saying that most women of my generation don't have to experience empty-nest depression because they have careers and interests beyond their families—and thank goodness for modern conveniences! I'm fortunate to be a part of that demographic.

Parenting is a time-consuming and hard-work adventure no matter what era. We should be joyous when the last offspring leaves the nest. We did well. So, here's a great whoop of joy and a hearty hallelujah, not just for myself, but also for the generations that went before me.

Girls! Here's to us!

—*Lesson Learned*: I still love my kids, but I've learned to put my feet up—and feel good about it.

A Heavenly Nudge

Shirley Thompson

When I was a small child, I saw a woman standing in front of our house watching me. I had been told since infancy that I had been adopted, and when I saw the woman I knew deep down inside that she was my "other" mother.

I had been adopted by the most wonderful, caring parents any child could want. As I grew up I was loved and happy and had no real desire to find my birth family, although my adoptive mother gave me many "clues" along the way. She even gave me a newspaper picture of the doctor who had delivered me and tucked it into my baby book in case I one day wanted to learn more about my birth family.

From my adoption papers I knew that I had been named Rosemary Lillian, although I was renamed Shirley. Over the years, and after several moves, I had lost all the clues my mother had so lovingly saved for me.

In my "second" fifty years, God had something very wonderful in store for me. When my youngest daughter was expecting her first child—my first grandchild—she began to encourage me to look for my birth family.

I had heard of a group in Illinois called Truth Seekers in Adoption, and I contacted them. But I was certain they would never find anything since, after all, it had been over fifty years. But they succeeded.

They found that my birth mother had passed away the previous fall, but they gave me her widower's name and address. They also helped me get a copy of her obituary and I found that she had three other children. When you have been an only child for more than half a century, that takes some getting used to!

Not long after, I saw a show on television about adoption and felt I was being nudged into doing something. I called my mother's widower and learned that my mother had a sister in Arizona and a brother in Alaska.

Later, I felt the nudge again, a little stronger. I dialed information in Alaska and managed to get my uncle's number. I called, but he was away on a trip. Then I called Arizona and got my aunt Rose's number. I talked with her and she and I exchanged letters. She sent me a group picture of herself with her brother and sisters. I was stunned when I turned over the photo and saw the names of my mother's sisters: Rose, Mary, and Lillian! My name at birth: Rosemary Lillian.

Word spread to the traveling uncle and to my sisters and brother. Within a year there was a family reunion as well as a wedding. I met so many cousins! And if I had to pick people to be my blood relatives, I couldn't have done better.

So even though I had glimpsed my mother only

once, standing in front of my house, I was given the opportunity through the children she raised to realize what a special person she was.

—*Lesson learned:* There is nothing like family! It had to be God who nudged me and enriched my second fifty years beyond belief.

A Breath of Fresh Air
Peggy Bruce

One day my husband, our adult daughter, and I were sitting at our breakfast bar talking. I no doubt was telling him the error of his ways when my daughter said quietly, "Breathe in, Dad; breathe out." It was like someone hit me upside the head. I realized instantly what she was saying!

We all learn by what we see and hear as we grow up, and it took me lo these many years to realize that I had followed my mother's example and had become a "smotherer." I thought it was my duty to give my opinions and thoughts on all aspects of my family's day-to-day living—whether they asked for it or not. In so doing I was simply carrying on my mother's same irritating and sometimes destructive habit, which had bugged me and other family members for as long as I can remember. She was a champion smotherer!

Once I discovered this "inherited" character flaw (isn't it convenient that we can blame our parents for our faults!), I was amazed that my two children still loved me. The patience they demonstrated should have earned a blue ribbon for each one of them.

While I was not zapped by a thunderbolt, this sudden awakening transformed me into a woman content to let her husband and her grown children live their own lives. And my new enlightened attitude continues to evolve each day. From the instant of that breakfast bar revelation I determined to do my best not to be a smothering kind of mother or wife. I must admit, however, that giving up old ways is difficult and sometines I slip and offer advice as opinion. On the lighter side, I can get a laugh almost anytime by calling, "Don't forget your jacket!" or "Be sure to tell them . . ."

I find that it truly is grand to be concerned only with my own life. (The burden is not so heavy when you are telling just yourself what to do instead of several people!) I find I have much more time to spend on things that benefit me, and, in the long run, benefit them as well. I have evolved into a more calm person, and I like myself a lot better for this major change I have made in my life.

—*Lesson learned*: Mothering does not mean smothering!

The Papier-Mache Plane
Ellen Javernick

I found it today. The papier-mache airplane my son Matt made so long ago. He was in kindergarten then. Now both Matt and Mike, his older brother, are grown and I'd been going through their outgrown treasures.

Memories flooded back as I looked at the plane Matt had worked on so diligently. He'd spent many mornings in the basement by himself. First he rolled newspaper to form the wings and body. He used half a roll of masking tape to fasten them together before he mixed up the wallpaper paste. The paste was carefully stirred so no lumps would spoil the finished surface. How patiently Matt had waited the three days for the plane to dry. He dribbled a little when he painted, but the red and yellow sort of mixed together and made a nice camouflage orange.

We discussed the propeller, which he finally decided to cut from a margarine tub lid. He fastened it in place so the propeller would "really spin." At last, the airplane was finished. He was proud of it and decided to take it to school for show-and-tell that very afternoon.

As the morning progressed, his confidence seemed to fade. Maybe it wasn't really so good. "Will the kids think it's dumb?" he asked me. I tried to reassure him, but perhaps because he'd had to ask for it, he thought my praise was insincere. Then, shortly before lunch he told me he didn't think he'd show the plane after all. He set it down on the dining room table.

It was still there when Mike came home for lunch. Mike was in third grade and Matt thought his older brother knew everything. Mike picked up the airplane and smiled approvingly. "Hey, Matt, this is neat!"

"Ya really think so?" asked Matt.

"Yup," said Mike.

Nothing more was said about the plane while the boys ate their lunch, but when they set off for school, I noticed that Matt was carrying his plane. Mike's simple, unsolicited praise told Matt that the plane was really good. It not only helped Matt that day, but it had a lasting effect on his self-esteem.

—*Lesson learned:* My grown sons won't need the papier-mache plane, but I tucked it back into the drawer to remind me of the power of praise.

Tea and Conversation
Mary M. Harper

My granddaughter and I gave a party. She made the invitations with a little help, and together we made plans for the special event. The day before, I carefully washed the antique china that belonged to my husband's grandmother, and my granddaughter polished the silver spoons. The anticipation was almost too much for an eight-year-old girl.

A trip to the bakery was special. We looked at the wonderful dainty cookies and finally chose four kinds for our tea party.

The day of the party, my granddaughter set the tea table using the china and silver spoons, laying them out on an embroidered cloth. Everything was perfection.

Waiting for three o'clock was almost unbearable. We had invited my granddaughter's younger sister, her mother, and her great-grandmother. They all arrived exactly at the appointed hour and the tea party began.

We sipped tea, ate tiny cookies, and carried on polite conversation. The children loved acting grown up, and the grownups loved acting like children. The party was a big success.

——*Lesson Learned:* I have learned from my granddaughter to have fun doing simple things I had long ago forgotten. I have learned how much pleasure one can receive from helping a child learn and experience new things—whether it is lessons from a school book or learning the social graces.

Grandmothers and little girls go together like tea and cookies.

A Listening Ear

Shelley Peterman Schwarz

When I was a little girl, my father told me that one of the reasons he fell in love with my mother was because she was such a good listener. I had lots of opportunities to be around my parents, because they owned a restaurant and I worked there. One of my mother's many jobs was to seat customers, and I watched her listen to them as well as to employees and delivery people when they shared personal stories. My mom's warmth and friendly and accepting manner were a real asset to the business.

I never thought about the significance of my father's words or my mother's actions until a few years ago. My increasing disability due to multiple sclerosis had taken its toll over the years. I retired as a teacher, started using a three-wheeled, battery-operated wheelchair, and I relinquished my driver's license. Every day I gave up another piece of my independence, and my worries were not just about what my illness was doing to my body, but also about what it was doing to my relationships with family and friends.

Today I have no use of my legs or right arm and hand, and only minimal use of my left hand. Yet my life is wonderful!

My husband and I have been happily married for

thirty-one years and our two grown children are exceptionally caring and compassionate. As for my friends, they don't come any better! I couldn't do without them. They help me dress, prepare meals, get me in and out of bed, keep appointments, run errands, and support me in every way they can.

How could I be so lucky? I could never "repay" these wonderful people for all they have done and continue to do for me. Every day I marvel at their commitment.

It wasn't until my fiftieth birthday (a day I never thought I'd live to see) that I realized that maybe the reason my life was so blessed was directly related to what my father found so special in my mother: that she was such a good listener. Maybe as a role model she taught me to be the same.

Today everyone is so busy running through life they simply don't have time to stop and truly listen to anyone. Since I can't race, I have the time to lend a listening ear.

—*Lesson learned*: Perhaps the most important lesson I've learned in my first fifty years is the reason why we have been given two ears but only one mouth: we should listen twice as much as we talk. It's one of the best ways we can respect and reward all those people who make a difference in our lives.

Here Comes Ruth!

Ruth S. Jung

Usually after I have entered the front door and passed through the entryway, one of the ladies will see me walking into the dining room and excitedly announce my entrance by shouting at the top of her voice, "Here comes Ruth!"

Following that introduction I am touched by the chorus of voices around the room: "Hi, Ruth!" or "Good morning, Ruth!" or "So good to see you, Ruth!"

This is Senior Manor in Sparta, Illinois, a nursing home where I was supervisor for twenty years. Even though I retired a few years ago, on each of my frequent visits there I take pleasure in the royal welcome I receive from the wonderful people who were residents during my tenure. It is good to see them and check on their progress and to chat about the "old times" we had together.

It is this type of recognition that has given me the will and determination to survive my own physical problems—a heart condition and cancer.

An even stronger force driving my determination to add more years to my life is my grandson, Kyle. He is thirteen as I write this, but was only two when I had major heart surgery. I vowed to come through the operation in order to see Kyle grow up. As I write this eleven years later, obviously I succeeded (for which I thank God).

Since that traumatic experience and other health problems, I have forged ahead not only seeing my grandson grow up but *helping* him grow up. I started by taking him (and his bottle) to church when he was still a little tyke; later I took him on a bus trip to the St. Louis Zoo. We also visited other nearby attractions, a Science Center, underground caverns, and, still later, along with my daughter, drove to Washington, D.C., for sightseeing and, of course, made a special trip to Disney World.

Kyle plays the saxaphone and takes piano lessons. He plays baseball at school, and I try to attend as many games as possible. His interest in baseball naturally means that he and I try to take in at least one game each summer in St. Louis to see the Cardinals play.

So I have kept my vow to see him grow up, and I am thankful for the time I have been given to share with him. I would say the feelings between Kyle and me are mutual: he thinks as much of me as I do of him. So, since I have made it this far, my goal now is to see him in college!

I'm happy to say that my granddaughter Stacey, with whom I share a warm mutual fondness, recently presented me with a delightful great-grandson. So today I have still another compelling reason to keep forging ahead! I guess I enjoy being around and needed by the young as well as the old.

Many of the nursing home residents tell me the place hasn't been the same since I left. I recognize this as flattery—Senior Manor is still a wonderful place—but I am happy to hear it, because my heart and soul are still there.

I know that one of these years I'll have to "retire" from Kyle, too. But I'm betting Grandma Ruth will be at his college graduation!

—*Lesson learned:* Keep your thinking positive—it's great longevity medicine!

To My First Grandchild

Little one,
I have waited so long and wondered
What it would be like to be a grandmother.
It is strange that you, yet unborn, can teach me.
But you have.

It is in anticipation of your coming
That I understand His plan for life's circle.
Now I know that the timeless miracle of our bond
Is that I will be your yesterdays
As you are my tomorrows.

—Jean Moyer

EIGHT

SPECIAL VIEWS

Bow down thine ear, and hear the words
of the wise, and apply thine heart unto
my knowledge.
—Proverbs 22: 17–18

Have a Good Day
Laurie Boulton

It was another shopping day at Publix, and again I noticed the disheveled man in the handicapped parking place by the entrance. Seated in a rickety lawn chair and surrounded by bulging garbage bags, he greeted shoppers as they passed.

This time, instead of shunning him, I approached this presumably homeless man. "Hello, and God bless," I heard through a toothless smile. Thinking he was "begging," I dug into my purse for a special two-dollar bill I carried. Dropping it in his styrofoam cup (his coffee cup!), I wished him a happy Thanksgiving.

Thank you," he said. "You're very kind."

We conversed awhile each week after that, and "Pop" (as I learned all regular shoppers fondly called him) explained that he biked twice a week to the parking lot to collect the aluminum cans people brought him to recycle. Although many people assumed he was homeless, he wasn't. He was eighty-five and a World War II veteran who loved people and stayed young interacting with them.

We began a two-year friendship in that parking space. Each week I looked forward to Pop's friendly greeting. He greeted me by name, asked about my family and recalled our every conversation. Pop encouraged me with my poetry writing. He gave me permission to take photographs of him and eagerly awaited his duplicate copies to add to his one frayed black-and-white Army photo.

I felt badly that I had once avoided him because of his appearance. Pop pedaled by our condo early in the morning on the berm of a busy road to the shopping center. After the sun grew high, he loaded his cans into his bike baskets and made the three-mile trip home. I worried about his safety, although he wore a neon orange vest and had a flag attached to his bicycle.

Pop's "Have a good day" greetings were infectious. When greeted by name, hurried shoppers often stopped to say hello. Once I saw a man drive up during a rain shower and hand Pop a golf umbrella, calling out, "Have a good day." Another shopper helped Pop attach it to his lawn chair, and Pop was dry every rainy day thereafter!

Recently, due to complications from an accident and old age, Pop left us. Among other things, he left me with fond memories of human kindness, and he taught me the importance of greeting people by name and using that name in conversation. The ripple effect of his congenial personality continues to reward me. And I received it all in exchange for my special two-dollar bill.

—*Lesson learned*: Never judge a book by its cover: go ahead and open up the pages.

A Joy Forever
Mary H. McAllister

It was daybreak, and as the space shuttle lifted off the launch pad and angled out over the Atlantic, I kept repeating, "Beautiful!" "Beautiful!" "Beautiful!" Then I suddenly realized that not everyone would share my conception of beauty. To them, perhaps, they were simply witnessing the technological miracle that it was: a streaking flash across the sky.

They might not agree with me that of all the gorgeous, magnificent and majestic things on earth, the ocean, and its surroundings are the ultimate. Would they agree that wolves, lions, and tigers are beautiful? The mountains, a waterfall, a rose—all remind me of what a beautiful world God has created.

Obviously, I was learning after age eighty the truth in the old saying, "Beauty is in the eye of the beholder."

How could anyone else call my dog, Frisky, attractive? He has the reputation of being the ugliest dog in the world. Every day is a bad-hair day for him. His hair is coarse, stands up in all directions, and is an odd shade of dirty blonde. Because of his whiskers and his long legs, one of my friends called him a billy goat. Another friend (mistakenly, I hope) called him Scruffy. But he loves me!

He follows me around from room to room and lies at my feet under my desk. He sits in the chair with me and "helps" me read the newspaper each morning. I am sure he would be glad to share my coffee if I would let him. If he misses me, he will peek around the corner to check my whereabouts.

After eighty-one years of never allowing a dog on my bed, I have relented, and he snores right along with me! Even with his arthritis, his starved appearance due to a pancreatic condition, and looking as though I never feed him, I catch myself believing that he is indeed beautiful.

—*Lesson learned*: I see Frisky in the line by Keats: "What the imagination seizes as beauty, must be truth."

As Young As You Feel
Ron Wiggins

Friends of Bayley Poole who work with her at Gwen Burge Realty in Lake Worth [Florida], have entreated me to write a custom-made "you know you are fifty" [newspaper] column to appear on her birthday, as a surprise.

Well, the surprise is on you, friends of Bayley Poole. I'm running the column you requested now, while she's still forty-nine. How do you know? She may decide to postpone number fifty until she feels she's "ready."

And anyway, I don't know anything about being 50—unless it's something like being $48^{11}/_{12}$. What I do know is that the older you get, the more ages you can be. If you're seventy, you can be any age up to seventy. But if you are ten, you can only be ten because you don't know how to be older.

Some examples will show you what I mean.

When my mom immerses herself in her genealogy studies, she is building on her fondly recalled conversations with her parents and grandparents, uncles and aunts. During her studies, every new revelation I am sure comes not to my sixty-nine-year-old mother but to a girl of ten listening raptly to tales of how her grandmother came to Jacksonville on a buckboard and how her grandfather piloted a riverboat the length of the St. Johns River.

When my dad works on his model railroad land-scape, who is it building the mine shaft spur, the seventy-two-year-old patent attorney or the twelve-year-old child of the Depression who had to postpone hobby shop dreams?

Our friends the Gilmores are retired now, but have every intention of taking their annual three-week motorcycle trip up through New England and Nova Scotia. Their children are grown and have children of their own, but have the Gilmores really left their thirties behind? I don't think so.

My friend Greg, forty-four, has been flying more than two years, certainly enough for the novelty to wear off. And yet if I should call him tonight and say, "How about flying to Fort Myers tonight, shooting some touch-and-go landings and coming straight back?" he would say, "Only if you twist my arm. I'll be in your driveway in two minutes with my sleeve rolled up." As enthusiasm levels go, Greg is eighteen.

Whenever I get a good book, I try to loan it to my friend Porter, sixty-seven, before I read it, because he pencils his own comments in the margins. It's fun seeing the passages that impress him and knowing that ideas excite his imagination. Porter has the outlook of a twenty-seven-year-old doctoral candidate just hitting his stride.

Most mornings when I leave the house, my wife, Nellie, is slugging tennis balls with men students ten and fifteen years her junior, and I marvel at her grace and agility. And when I return home in the afternoon, she may be offering a strategy lesson to a group or pounding balls with an advanced student. According to her driver's license, she turned fifty a couple of years ago, but I think somebody forgot to tell her body.

As for myself, I will turn fifty next March, and as for getting old, that'll have to wait until after I've completed my home harmonica course, reread Twain and Dickens, gotten *some* proficiency in Spanish, broken 80 on the golf course, earned a state tennis ranking, and learned to ski.

One piece of advice if you decide to go ahead and turn fifty, Bayley Poole: you may find yourself disappointed at class reunions. Some of those people are so old they won't recognize you.

[—*Lesson learned:*] The older you get, the more ages you can be.

Editor's note: This column appeared in the *Palm Beach Post.* We let Wiggins, who was just under fifty when he wrote the column, slip into our collection because he has since met our age requirement and is even more convinced today that you're as young as you feel.

My Silent Self
Marlene Brown

We were having dinner when the telephone rang. My husband George answered and talked for a few minutes, then hung up and announced that his company unexpectedly needed him for a week in New York to handle a special assignment. Not much time to make arrangements and pack, but his good news was that I could accompany him, do some shopping, take in a play, visit the Guggenheim, or whatever: business for him but an unexpected vacation for us—all expenses paid. We both sparked to the prospect and George poured us an after-dinner drink to celebrate. He was just a few months away from retirement, so this could be our last opportunity to enjoy such an expense-free trip together.

Our children were grown and gone, so I had no reason not to go, but while thinking about the idea over the next hour or two I began to have reservations. I had always been an active individual, involved in community and volunteer activities, packing the kids off to school, working part-time. I was always "with" people, talking to people, phoning people, helping people. Did I honestly need a trip from Los Angeles to New York to mingle with more people? For some reason I had been feeling strangely ill at ease lately. Perhaps more than a trip, I needed some time alone. Maybe even try to discover myself.

After finishing our nightcap I was relaxed enough to tell George that I had decided to stay behind and be by myself for a week. He was disappointed but seemed to understand.

This was my opportunity, after years of being driven almost exclusively by "outside" forces around me, to focus on my feelings and strengths somewhere inside me.

It took a day or two after George left for me to realize that I did not have to answer the phone and could let it ring. I let the TV remain silent and left the car in the garage. In the following days I learned that inner peace had to be nurtured slowly and could not be found on the outside, and not in self-indulgence.

In my new peaceful surroundings I came to realize that self-gratifications never last long. A new purchase. A new kiss. They all pass. I learned for the first time the wisdom in the saying that accumulating worldly goods, rather than paving the road to tranquility, actually instills fear because they might be stolen. I was beginning to get comfortable with myself.

Call it a spiritual awakening or soaring with the angels, this was a taste of real freedom, not a time of constant suffocation by air filled with voices—so irritable at times—which, oddly enough, I often sought to fill my inner void.

By the time George returned (and the seven days had

passed) I felt I was on the road to becoming a more complete woman. My decision to spend time alone introduced me to the space between silence and wisdom, and the discovery of endless possibilities. It required will, and especially patience and discipline. I am grateful for having taken that journey.

—*Lesson learned*: Silence is golden. I'm going to try it more often!

First Impressions
Steven J. Lesko, Jr.

It was an unusually warm day in May as I was returning home from running errands. As I approached my house, I noticed two teenagers sitting at the end of my drive-way, enjoying a cigarette under the cool shade of a tree. They were sporting "alternative" hairstyles and clothing, both of which I considered untraditional at best. When I activated the garage door opener, the noise startled the young men who quickly got to their feet.

They were excitedly trying to say something to me which I couldn't hear. I rolled down my car window and heard them exclaim apologetically, "We're going, mister!" I told them that they were welcome to stay. They thanked me politely and resumed what they were doing.

After I went into the house I noticed them still chatting and sitting on the asphalt, which didn't look terribly comfortable. I went out to them and asked if they wouldn't be more comfortable sitting on the porch chairs, and offered them a soda. The boys accepted my offer with thanks and I left to finish some chores, telling them to leave the empty cans on the porch.

When I returned, the boys were gone and the two empty cans were on the porch. In the ring of one of the cans were two one-dollar bills rolled up along with a note written on a piece of paper from their cigarette pack. It said: "Dear Kind Sir: Thank you for letting us use your porch and for the pop. This would be a much better place if everyone was just like you. Here is $2 for your kindness. God bless you, Dave and Justin."

I was touched by the simple sincerity of their note and I wished that somehow I could return their money to them. Luckily, one day as I was relaxing on my porch, I noticed Dave and Justin walking by the house and I waved for them to join me. I gave them their money back, along with another soda. We proceeded to chat about what they were doing and what their future plans were. Throughout our conversation I was struck by the politeness and respect they showed me.

After they had gone, I went into the house. Later, when I went back onto the porch I found a dollar bill on the floor, presumably for the soda.

I thought of how easy it would have been to turn these young men away solely because of their appearance.

—Lesson learned: I learned that a responsive heart can exist at any age, under any outward trappings.

Know Thyself

Nova N. Barnett

When my brother phoned to tell me that he was accepting a position in a small Alaska bush town, I immediately told him I wanted to go along. Of course, those close to me thought I had lost my mind. "After all," they said, "You're almost fifty years old. No one just picks up and starts over at that age!"

Actually, I had been continually starting over. I had traveled abroad and had visited almost every state and had lived in most. I had graduated from a university, worked for the Atomic Energy Commission in California, taught dancing in New York City, and even appeared on a regularly scheduled television show.

The one thing I had not accomplished was finding out just who I really was.

I stayed seven years in bush Alaska and that was longer than I had stayed in any one place in my entire life. In the small town where I lived we had no doctor, no telephones, no roads, no hair-dresser. In fact, we had almost none of the creature comforts to which I had been accustomed, and without which most people feel they cannot survive. What we did have, however, were thousands of miles of pristine beauty, unspoiled by human inhabitants, and wildlife galore.

Nothing can compare to the magnificence of a Rose-of-Sharon sticking its lovely head up through an Alaskan snowbank in late April. Nothing could be more thrilling than to watch a mother bear bring her young to the river to teach them how to forage for food. Nothing can be more awe-inspiring than to look out your window and see majestic mountains that seem to go on forever.

Nothing could be more impressive than to sit beside a river during the spring thaw and see it rushing to the sea with such fervor that it trips over itself. And nothing could be more frightening than enduring the long harsh winters that seem especially designed to test the mettle of the most stalwart.

Did I recognize the lessons I was learning while I lived in Alaska? Certainly not. But when I returned to "the lower forty-eight," I felt more self-assured and more confident, but I did not know why, nor did I try to understand. I'm not that smart.

A few years later, I was watching a television re-run of *Designing Women* in which the four stars were talking about going on a vacation together. One of the women (played by Delta Burke) stated that she did not want to go. When asked why, she said, "I have learned that no matter where you go, there you are."

At that very moment, I knew the most important lesson Alaska had taught me. In fact, the greatest lesson I have ever learned: you are who you are no matter where you go. And if you don't like yourself, you must change—at any age—to get the most out of life.

—*Lesson learned:* Learn to live successfully with yourself, whether you reside in the bustling canyons of a big city, the peaceful suburbs, rural America, or the remote expanse of bush. Thank you, Alaska; you were a great tutor!

Alone in a Croweded City
Nina Kluger

My relatives and friends thought I was out of my mind to attempt a trip halfway around the planet by myself, particularly because of my "advanced years." They each reminded me that Sydney, Australia, was a very long way from Florida, USA!

My husband and I were habitual travelers. We had been to all fifty states and a good part of Canada, as well as a few trips to Europe, touching on parts of Asia and Africa. When he passed away I figured it was the end of my sightseeing, and for a while I limited my travels to visiting my daughter not too far away. But I missed going to new places and venturing into the unknown.

My big opportunity to "break out" came when my older son Philip moved temporarily to Australia to help establish a horse ranch. I saved vigorously for a year to go there for a visit.

Luckily, en route I had an old friend living in Los Angeles, and I visited with her for a few days before boarding the long 14½-hour Qantas flight to Sydney. There I transferred to a commuter plane to Newcastle, about a hundred miles north, then took a taxi to my motel.

The following morning, friends of Philip picked me

up and we drove out into the horse country where he was working. Of course we had a joyous reunion.

As Phil was working during the week, I had pre-planned four days of sightseeing in Sydney. My room was at a five-star skyscraper hotel overlooking the beautiful harbor and the famous opera house with its billowing sails. The concierge obtained a ticket for me for the next evening's performance, and as the opera area is somewhat on the order of a theme park, I went there early and spent a good part of the day wandering about the esplanades. The following two days I continued sightseeing and took different harbor cruises. However, I was happy to fly back to Newcastle and spend the second weekend with my son before returning home.

Although I'm glad I went to Sydney, I felt alone and bored with myself. Whoever coined "Lonely in the midst of crowds" was so very right. In my mind, the whole concept of being a tourist was to share new experiences with others. Perhaps that was the worst: not having someone to share things with.

For me, traveling alone was a totally new experience interspersed with ups and downs. I now realize that I must accept my once-again-single status as being different—because it comes at an entirely different time in my life.

—*Lesson learned*: My next foreign adventure will be with a group or with friends, in order to share and to remember—together.

See You in the Morning
Elyse Kaner

Although I didn't realize it at the time, my Grandma Lena was one of my greatest teachers.

She came to live with us in 1952 after Grandpa died. Our house in Superior, Wisconsin, got a little crowded, with my two sisters and me sharing a room, but we didn't mind at all.

My grandparents had a secondhand store on the other side of town, and when Grandpa died, Grandma ran the store. She was spry for her age and thought nothing of climbing those high ladders to satisfy a customer's query about an old smock or a checkered flannel shirt.

Grandma was from the Old Country and spoke in broken English, but she had no trouble being understood. She also spoke several languages, a reputation that brought a lot of foreign visitors to her store.

A short, handsome woman, blessed with curly silver hair, Grandma could brighten any room with her smile. She also brightened my days.

I was six when she moved in. It was my job to wash the breakfast dishes, and I hated it. One day I moaned and groaned until she graciously offered to do them.

That's when I learned one of the lessons. Grandma

performed the task with joy! She was glad to have hands to do the dishes with and was grateful for the food that had been on those dishes. "A lot of dishes means a lot of people in the house enjoying food together," she added.

Every night before bedtime, I visited Grandma's room wearing my pajamas. We'd play Chinese checkers, or she would practice English while I worked on the Hebrew she was teaching me. When I got tired, I'd say, "Good night, Grandma. I'll see you in the morning."

She always replied, "I hope so."

Grandma was grateful for each day and for having a roof over her head that she shared with those she loved.

Every time she came into the house, she'd put her hand on the mezuzah, a small scroll with Biblical passages hung on door frames to bless and protect the home. Then she'd bring her hand to her lips and say, "Hom, sweet hom." To this day, whenever I enter my home, I touch the mezuzah, kiss my hand and say, "Home, sweet home."

One day when Grandma was in her eighties, my mother was visiting at a neighbor's house and saw fire engines rush by. Grandma had forgotten about a pot of water she was heating for tea and it boiled over. Frightened when she saw the smoke, Grandma called the fire department.

A few open windows solved the problem, but a question remained. Grandma rarely used the phone because she was embarassed by her broken English, so how did she find and dial the number so fast?

It turned out Grandma had been carrying the fire department number in her sweater pocket for years, just in case.

Grandma worked six days a week until she was eighty-six years old. Then I guess she just got tired. When I visited her in the hospital she continued to teach me. Knowing she was near the end of her life, Grandma, who thought of others before herself, said, "Give my black coat to someone who needs it."

When I left the hospital that day, I said to Grandma, as I had so many times before, "Good night, Grandma. I'll see you in the morning."

As always, Grandma replied, "I hope so." She passed away that night, leaving me with the lifelong gift of her wisdom.

—*Lesson learned*: In addition to many other teachings, I'll always remember a special piece of advice that Grandma passed along: Your husband or your wife should always be your best friend.

Savin' My Love for You

Shirley Barksdale

We met on a blind date, and before the evening ended I knew that this handsome, sexy airline pilot was a pack rat.

At the restaurant, the theater, and all stops in between, he loaded his pockets with trivia: toothpicks, matchboxes (he didn't smoke), empty popcorn boxes. In his car, the overstressed glove compartment spewed broken golf tees, peanut shells, gum wrappers, and a broken yo-yo. Before I could ask, he said, "You never know when you might need something."

I married him anyway, certain that the love of a good woman would change him. But later, when I discovered that his "treasures" had accompanied us on one move after another, I cut the sweet talk and turned into a relentless nag. Nothing moved him. His stuff continued to grow and spread like cholera.

It took his mother, a formidable octogenarian, to bring him to his knees. She moved into an assisted-living facility and instructed him to ready the old home for the market. Never mind that she lived in Dallas and we lived in Denver.

Unfortunately, she too was afflicted with the pack-rat gene, and a lifetime of collecting had generated much hostility and many threats from the homeowners' association, the Sanitation Department, and the county sheriff, all of whom she blithely ignored. To her credit she had the good sense to move out while she could still find the front door.

We rented a dumpster and hired a crew of burly workers, who defected immediately when they saw the floor-to-ceiling debris. I defected right along with them. In the end, it became solely my husband's unenviable task. He spent all his vacation and layover time commuting between Denver and Dallas to clean, haul, and swear.

"What a terrible way to live!" he mumbled while recuperating on sick leave. I assured him I knew the feeling.

His vow to give up hoarding should have made me rhapsodic, except that he replaced it with another strange compulsion. He became a neat freak. He tossed out everything not in its usual place. However, this phase ended abruptly when he threw out, then retrieved from the garbage, an ancient "brain bag" (pilot-speak for flight bag, so named for its survival data—the Jeppesen Airway Manual, Instrument Approach Procedure, and a rabbit's foot).

Curious to know why this particular bag had caused his pack-rat syndrome to resurface, the minute he left town I traced it to the tool shed. I found that it held my love letters to him. They logged the important events of our cluttered years, from that blind date to a recent valentine.

I carried the bag to the attic where I kept my own private "collection" in a hat box. In it were his love letters to me. Among them were hurried notes, bits of sentimental poetry he had tucked under my breakfast place when he left at dawn. The anniversary cards still had the power to make my heart race.

Any man, I decided, who could express so much love with such constancy to a nagging wife is a man to be cherished. I cleaned up the old flight bag, dusted off the old hat box and snuggled them side by side on a shelf in our bedroom closet. There I could see them every day and be reminded that some things are worth hoarding—like love, for instance.

—*Lesson learned*: I learned that love is never clutter.

Shoes Not Required
Dixie Darr

I have a problem handling authority and bureaucracy. That's why it took me three colleges, six majors, and twelve years to earn a bachelor's degree. I dropped out so many times that I lost count; I made dropping out an art form.

Naive and arrogant, I thought learning was simply too important to leave it in the hands of others. Like Albert Einstein, I believed "the only thing that interferes with my learning is my education."

I suppose I first made the distinction between learning and education in tenth grade, when I wrote a book report on *To Kill a Mockingbird*. My teacher, Miss Jacobs, asked me to focus on the difference between what Scout was taught and what she learned. That's when I realized that the really important learning occurred outside the classroom.

Anyway, after leaving Colorado State University following a miserable freshman year, I immersed myself in learning, reading voraciously and pretending that college didn't matter. These days, people like Bill Gates are positive role models for college dropouts. But let's assume— just for argument's sake—that I was no Bill Gates. I needed a degree.

I enrolled in college classes here and there, eventually completing a degree at the University of Colorado at Denver. After taking a few years off to recover from my ordeal in formal education, I wandered back up to Fort Collins just long enough to pick up a Master's degree in lifelong learning. Then I promptly stopped taking classes.

Instead, I started teaching at the University of Phoenix. You may think it's a strange choice of professions, until you understand that my students are adults who, for one reason or another, didn't go to college the traditional way. What I teach them is how to convert what they've learned outside a classroom into college credit.

Miss Jacobs would be proud.

To become a true master of any subject, you have to learn about it from all sides. Although I had designed Web-based courses and taught online for several years, I had never taken an online class. So, recently, I became a virtual student myself. I took courses on Web page designing, an online faculty training course, even a free class on the Beatles. I did it all from my home computer, on my own schedule, with no hassles about traffic or parking or sitting for long hours in uncomfortable chairs. It was fun, and I didn't even have to wear shoes.

My freshman classes at CSU were decidedly not fun. Maybe that's why most students seemed to be majoring in drinking and carousing.

That was in 1966. Funny, isn't it, how little things have changed since then? Will Rogers had a great idea for getting students interested. "Instead of giving money to found colleges to promote learning," he said, "why don't they pass a constitutional amendment prohibiting anybody from learning anything? If it works as good as the Prohibition one did, why, in five years we would have the smartest race of people on Earth."

Until the legislature wises up, the Internet has that illicit feel about it. I'm now checking out online piano lessons. After that, who knows? I've always wanted to study physics, Spanish, art, religion, yoga, and dozens of other subjects.

—*Lessons learned:* Thanks to the Internet, control over my learning is back where it belongs: in my own hands, right at my fingertips.

Open Your Eyes

Jackie McLean

[Jackie McLean was a good friend of fellow jazz saxophonist, the all-time great Charlie "Bird" Parker. In 1999, nearing eighty, McLean took a look back at a lesson he learned—and relearned:]

One day in '48 or '49, I ran into Bird on Broadway. It happened to be the day of Hot Lips Page's funeral. Bird had known him in Kansas City. He said, "Where you goin'? Why don't you come with me uptown?" So I went with him up to 145th Street. He said he wanted to view Page's body. We went to the funeral parlor and signed the book, went up to the casket and looked down at him, and he said, "Boy, he sure looks good." He said, "Page was really a great trumpet player." We just looked at him.

And then we walked on Eighth Avenue through Harlem from 145th Street down to 125th Street. He was looking in windows. I remember we looked in the fish store where all the fish were lying in the window on ice, and he said, "Wow, look at that. Isn't that beautiful?" And I said, "What?" You know, I was looking at fish lying on ice. He said, "Don't you see all the colors?" I looked at where the sun was shining through the window onto their scales, and suddenly there were all these colors in front of me—purples and yellows and reds and blues and greens and silvers. I couldn't believe it.

[—*Lesson learned:*] I didn't see them at all until he said, "Look at the colors."

Suddenly

Sometimes I wonder why my steps seem slow.
Then I remember that the year is 2001
And I have walked a long, long way.

And
I notice that there are creases around my mouth
Where only laugh lines used to be.
Then I remember
that I have had much about which to smile

Strange, I don't remember growing old
But suddenly, looking down,
I see my mother's hands folded in my lap.

Now
As I look back over the years
My heart overflows with remembering.
But when did I grow old?

—Jean Moyer

NINE

AFTER-50 WISDOM

Wisdom outweighs any wealth.
—Sophocles

Bits and Bytes of Wisdom

No tiptoeing allowed: Ernest Hemingway, who died at age sixty-two, was married four times. In his later years he indicated that he had finally learned a lesson about matrimony when he advised his son that marriage "goes on for a long time, and you should be faithful. It is not a step to be taken lightly."

Just say it: Ed Kofman, sixty-six, a Florida retiree, advises that "no matter what you're fighting about, the wife is always right and the guy always has to say, `I'm sorry.' Believe me, it hurts sometimes, but it's all they want to hear, and what's worth not saying it?"

Pour a glass of suds: Goldie Davage, whose grandmother was a cousin of abolitionist Frederick Douglass, began working as a maid for three dollars a week and eventually saved enough to buy her own house. She celebrated her one-hundredth birthday on January 1, 2000, with a party and a glass of beer. Davage was in almost perfect health and took no medication. She told friends that the real secret to her longevity was "a beer, a dance, and being able to smile at young men."

Two olives, please: Peg Bracken, author of *The I Hate to Cook Book*, published in 1960, opened her perennial bestseller with the never-to-be-forgotten declaration: "This book is for those of us who want to fold our dishwasher hands around a dry Martini instead of a wet flounder, come the end of a long day." Nonetheless, she did decades of cooking and her unintimidating and tasty recipes will be handed down for generations. At age eighty-one, she shared her thoughts on aging: "These are your declining years in which you can jolly well decline to do what you don't feel like doing, unless it makes you feel worse than doing it."

Play it safe: May Z. Cohen, a retired New York schoolteacher, suggests that you not be too hard on yourself and go easy on others. Praise at least 80 percent of the time, criticize less than 20 percent. "People say, `Tell it like it is.' That's bunk. If you tell it like it is, you won't have a wife or a husband or a friend."

Putting right along: Dora Goldberg is still an active golfer at eighty. She plays three times a week: Tuesday with a ladies league, eighteen holes on Friday, and nine holes on Sunday. Her advice: "Don't put things off. I started playing golf when I was fifty-five, and I just wish I had started earlier."

Listen up: Well-over-fifty Marcel Marceau doesn't speak often, but when he does he doesn't mince words. The world's most famous mime summed up his philosophy on life by saying, "It's good to shut up sometimes."

What? Me worry? In a magazine interview after reaching 102 years of age, George Dawson, the grandson of a slave, was asked to share the secret to his long, healthy life. "I never worry. Ever," he explained, "That's just trying to control other people and things that happen to you, and I know I can't do that. If you ask me, the reason most people get sick is that they worry too much."

Continuing Education—
To after Eighty

Margaret Kahn Garaway

I am happy to say that the best part of my life began after the age of fifty, when I learned not to be afraid of trying something new. It was in this spirit that I went off in 1970 with my husband Marty to the Navajo Reservation in Northeastern Arizona, where he had accepted a teaching position.

For most of his life, Marty had hoped to become a teacher. When he was fifty-two I finally convinced him to go back to college and earn his degree. Five years later he had his diploma in hand and was ready to go to work. However, there was a technical glitch: we were living in Los Angeles at the time, and they did not hire teachers over the age of fifty-five.

The good news was that the Bureau of Indian Affairs had no such age restriction, so without hesitation we packed up and headed for Arizona.

By the next year I was highly motivated to become a teacher myself. I plunged into the world of academia. Earlier, when I was in my forties, I had put off joining two friends in going to college because I felt I could not compete with young college students. But now I soon learned that because of my life's experiences my classes were not difficult.

In my junior year I was chosen the outstanding junior of the university and was invited to become a member of Phi Kappa Phi, a national honor society. With my BA degree in hand, having graduated summa cum laude, I decided to go on another year and get a Master's in teaching English as a second language.

Martin and I lived and taught on the Navajo Reservation for seventeen years. I became friends with the Navajo people and had the opportunity to learn and participate in many of their cultural activities. This experience inspired me to write my first book, *The Old Hogan*. It was published when I was sixty-eight. It is the story told by a house, which to the Navajo people represents the earth nurturing the family and its traditions. The book is considered a classic in the Southwest and has had nine printings.

At the age of seventy-six I began my own publishing company and published several books, some bilingual, which I had authored mostly for young readers. I have been speaking in schools, at writing conferences, and to adult groups since I was sixty-nine and I am still on the circuit at the age of eighty-three.

Martin began his seventeen-year Arizona career by first teaching Indian children in elementary school, then high schoolers and, ultimately, collegians at Northern Arizona University. In his eighties he ambitiously began a novel that he worked on for five years, but poor health interfered.

I knew Martin's novel was the fulfillment of a life-long dream, so I made a project of publishing it. The book, a thriller called *The Theft of the Anasazi Pots,* turned this eighty-six-year-old writer into an overnight sensation. The reader reponse was just the tonic he needed, and I'm sure it saved his life.

How wonderful that we both began new careers in our fifties; our lives gained a whole new dimension. We can look back with satisfaction on the work we did helping others.

—*Lesson learned:* I learned to try new things, to work
  aging to my advantage, and to reap the rewards.

Dance Like No One's Watching
Author Unknown

We convince ourselves that life will be better after we get married, have a baby, then another. Then we are frustrated that the kids aren't old enough and we'll be more content when they are. After that, we're frustrated that we have teenagers to deal with. We will certainly be happy when they are out of that stage.

We tell ourselves that our life will be complete when our spouse gets his or her act together, when we get a nicer car, are able to go on a nice vacation, when we retire.

The truth is, there's no better time to be happy than right now. Your life will always be filled with challenges. It's best to admit this to yourself. There will always be some obstacle in the way, something to be gotten through first, some unfinished business, time still to be served, a debt to be paid. These obstacles are your life. This perspective has helped me to see that there is no way to what is called happiness. Happiness is the way. So treasure every moment that you have. Treasure it more if you shared it with someone special, special enough to spend your time with . . . and remember that time waits for no one.

So stop waiting until you finish school, until you go back to school, until you lose ten pounds, until you

gain ten pounds, until you have kids, until your kids
leave the house, until you start work, until you retire,
until you get married, until you get divorced, until
Friday night, until Saturday morning, until you get a
new car or home, until your car or home are paid off,
until spring, until summer, until fall, until winter, until
you are off welfare, until the first or fifteenth, until your
song comes on . . . to decide that there is no better time
than right now to be happy.

[—*Lesson learned:*] Happiness is a journey, not a destina-
tion. Work like you don't need money, love like
you've never been hurt, and dance like no one's
watching.

Love Story—With a Waggly Tail
Bard Lindeman

I have fallen head over teakettle in love again, and in the autumnal years of my life. Since I work at home—and my wife doesn't—my lover and I see each other constantly. The giddy truth is that we're openly, unashamedly affectionate. We simply don't care who sees us.

Here's the biggest surprise—my wife doesn't give a fig. In truth, Jan believed from the outset that the athletic newcomer to our household would prove to be a boon, an elixir or tonic, to us both. She was right. For Nicky, our dark-eyed, floppy-eared, four-legged marvelous mutt is a lover to us both and a compelling reason to roll out of bed each morning.

In New Jersey, we had been cat people. But this was Georgia and we were going to have to change, so we set out to find ourselves a dog. We didn't know whether Nicky was a stray or an abandoned animal when we rescued him from the county animal shelter. He was cautious, even withdrawn, when he entered our home. My wife grew up on a north Georgia farm and remains an incorrigible animal lover. With a tinge of sadness in her voice, she asked, "Do you think he can become a loving pet? I mean, affectionate?"

I had no good answer at the time, yet I like to mimic

that question these nights when the Nickster—he answers to a variety of names—is sprawled high up on my wife's chest, his front paws just under her chin, and his adoring brown eyes locked onto her baby blues.

"If he were any more loving than he is," I tell her, "I'd have to sue for divorce."

By day, Nicky is my shadow, the barker-in-chief in our home, and the third leg on the family stool. Truth is, Nicky had used up his days as a county ward when we found him in his stark, flea-ridden cage. He was literally on doggie death row, awaiting a lethal injection, when we chose to bring this two-year-old, unpedigreed canine home. And each of his days is sweeter now because he escaped the animal executioner.

Through my reading and research, I've discovered that dogs are health mates as well as companions. Dog owners have lower blood pressure readings, lower blood cholesterol totals, and, overall, are less susceptible to heart disease than those who are dog-deprived. A University of California medical doctor, Judith Siegel, established that older adults who own pets visit their doctor 16 percent fewer times than those who don't have animal friends.

The faithful-dog (this can be read as one word) doesn't care if the master or mistress shuffles with athritis, has one chin too many, perhaps is past due on pesky credit card payments, or frequently forgets where the house keys were last seen.

My wife and I derive enormous comfort from loving our dog, who, we're convinced, was put on earth to make us laugh and feel good about our lives.

—*Lesson learned*: Dogs regularly boost our self-esteem and lure us out of emotional downturns. I urge you to invite a dog into your household. I can almost guarantee you'll feel better about yourself in a week's time.

Breaking the Age Barrier

Golda Meir served as prime minister of Israel from age seventy to seventy-five.

During World War II, Winston Churchill was the British prime minister from age sixty-five to seventy.

Noah Webster published two volumes of An *American Dictionary of the English Language* at age seventy.

Daniel Defoe was fifty-nine when he wrote *Robinson Crusoe*.

Actor and comic George Burns won his first Oscar at eighty.

Frank Lloyd Wright designed the Guggenheim Museum in New York City at ninety-one.

Giuseppe Verdi composed his operatic masterpiece *Otello* at age seventy-four and *Falstaff* at eighty.

Physician and humanitarian Albert Schweitzer was still performing operations at his African hospital at age eighty-nine.

Eleanor Roosevelt was sixty-one when President Truman appointed her to represent the United States as a delegate to the United Nations. She served until she was sixty-eight.

Mahatma Gandhi was seventy-seven when he successfully completed negotiations with Britain for the independence of India.

Dr. Seuss wrote *The Cat in the Hat* at fifty-three, and *You're Only Old Once* at age eighty-two.

Michelangelo was sixty-six when he finished painting the Sistine Chapel.

Casey Stengel didn't retire as manager of the New York Mets until he was seventy-five.

Grandma Moses didn't begin painting until she was eighty. She completed over 1,500 paintings after that; 25 percent of those were produced when she was past 100.

At age ninety-six, playwright George Bernard Shaw broke his leg when he fell out of a tree he was trimming in his backyard.

Doc Councilman, at fifty-eight, became the oldest person ever to swim the English Channel.

A DIFFERENT SOUND OF MUSIC
Victor Borge Remembered

Victor Borge will be remembered by legions of fifty-plussers as the keyboard genius who gave them countless laughs. He was the musical comedian whose sight gags and verbal quips entertained audiences of all ages throughout the world.

One of his gimmicks was to stumble into a Steinway, sounding a chord with his backside, and then confessing to the audience, "I play much better by ear, I can assure you."

He was trained in his early years for a career as a concert pianist, but instead turned to doing nightclub gigs because, as he explained it, he didn't have what a great pianist should have: the ability to apply the seat of the pants to the seat of the chair. He excelled at falling off the piano bench, much to the delight of his enthusiastic fans, managing at the same time to enthrall his listeners with his piano virtuosity.

In 1940, fate helped Mr. Borge, a Jew living in Denmark, escape the rising tide of Nazi persecution and terror. He went to the American Consulate in Stockholm and, as good luck would have it, one of the officers there turned out to be a fan of his. He was given a visa to Finland, where he literally was on the last boat leaving for the United States. "I got to the ship just as they were pulling up the gangplank," he told Harold C. Schonberg in an interview for the

New York Times. "It was the last boat to leave Finland for a long time."

Mr. Borge was the youngest of five sons of Bernhard Rosenbaum, a violinist with the Royal Danish Symphony. He was introduced to the piano by his mother at the age of three, and made his concert debut in Copenhagen when he was eight. As he matured, he became known in Scandinavia as a comic actor, composer, pianist, writer, and a director of movies, stage shows, and radio programs.

Following his trip from Finland, he arrived in the United States almost penniless and could not speak English. Mr. Borge taught himself the language by spending hundreds of hours in movie houses. He changed his name to Victor Borge and began performing in nightclubs.

In the 1950s, he set a Broadway record when his show, Comedy in Music, ran for 849 performances. It grossed more than $2 million.

His lesson learned might be summed up in a statement he made to Mr. Schonberg at the age of eighty: "I know life. I have had a full measure of experience. Shouldn't I take advantage of it? These days my acts are the essence of what I have accomplished. The fruit is on the tree. Should I let it rot?"

And when he was ninety, he was still performing about sixty shows a year and enjoying wider popularity through videotapes and CDs.

Victor Borge died in 2000 at the age of ninety-one.

Diet Right!

Frances Golden

My life changed dramatically shortly before I turned sixty, when my doctor handed me a strict diet. "Your triglycerides are so high they are completely out of range. There is no medication I can prescribe when the problem becomes as severe as yours. So dieting is the only route open to you at this stage." He paused for a moment and then said quite seriously, "Here is your `no-no' list. These are foods you cannot eat under any circumstances. If you want to live, follow this diet diligently."

His words cut through me like a knife, because no one enjoyed a hearty, no-foods-barred meal better than I. His stern warning had come in the aftermath of my suffering a pulmonary embolism, which is quite often fatal. So this dialogue was not a joke.

Noticing the pained expression on my face, the doctor said soothingly, "You may eat strawberries. They contain the least amount of sugar." Although this concession was charitable, it certainly didn't sound to me like the greatest goodie-replacement idea in the world.

So, it *was up to me?* What an unwelcome challenge. I had to find a solution to this "must-do" restriction.

Question: How do I do it? Answer: I must psyche myself out.

My mind ordered my body (and my mouth) to imagine that all the taboo foods on my list were not even a part of our earth. For my own benefit, this world was devoid of chocolate, pastries, candy, ice cream, fruit, meat, fried foods. Yes, even pizza.

Imagination was my only salvation, so I talked to myself, and, much to my surprise, I got answers. I told myself that Ben & Jerry did not even exist and had never concocted a single saturated fat–packed ice cream flavor. I denied that Mr. Heinz had ever dreamed up 57 varieties. In short, all my prohibited goodies simply did not exist. This new mindset became my life-saving approach to food control. I tested it over and over again, and soon had it working like a charm!

Thus, a short time after my visit with the doctor, when a group of my thoughtful friends placed a sixtieth birthday cake on the table in front of me, I put my psyche-out magic technique to work full throttle. As I looked down at the table, my mind envisioned a completely empty plate. There was no beautiful cake, no frosting, no "Happy Birthday, Fran" inscription, and no candles. Just a beautiful, clean, even crumbless, plate! Of course, as you can imagine, my hostess and all the guests were in total shock and disbelief when I asked for a tomato sandwich. (I found it hard to believe myself!)

Has my psyche-out approach continued to work?

Yes, indeed. I'm pleased to report that I recently celebrated my eighty-fifth birthday! The cake this time? Would you believe a butter-free, syrup-free, milk-free pancake?

—*Lesson learned:* The power of the mind is awesome. By taking "will power" one step further and making "no-no's" vanish, I was able to prolong my life—and you can do the same thing. (No, I don't think my technique can make your neighbor's yapping dog disappear!)

An Honest Answer
Norman Heberer

If your employer asks you what the employees in his company think about him, what do you say? Hedge a little? Say they think he is great when you know they don't feel that way at all? Tell the truth? How do you handle a hot potato like that?

That question was asked of me during an exit interview as I was leaving the company which had employed me for the previous seventeen years. I had not expected it.

I had joined this international company as an electrical engineer in their midwestern manufacturing plant. After I had been with them a few years, I became part of the "start-up team" that was sent to Brazil to handle construction of a new plant there, initiate the operation, and train personnel.

When this new facility was in full operation, the president approached me with an offer to return to the United States and help build and start up a new plant in California. I was excited with this advancement and opportunity. Sadly enough, the president was killed in an automobile accident, which resulted in the California project being canceled.

The new CEO was a very intelligent, capable, sensitive and basically friendly man, but somewhat aloof. His predecessor had been extremely friendly and made a point to visit each manufacturing facility on a regular basis—always being sure to speak with as many factory workers as possible (many on a first-name basis). Conversely, the new chief rarely visited any plants.

Shortly after this management change, I received an offer to assume a higher position in another company. In those days job-changing often carried a stigma and I wanted to make sure that I left the company under the best of circumstances. Hence, I requested an exit interview with the new CEO, whom I had come to know very well through the Brazilian and other projects.

On my last day of work, I went to his office for the interview. We had a pleasant talk and I thanked him for the experience I had gained in working for the company. He was very cordial, expressed regret that there were no similar openings for me within his company, and wished me success. Then, he surprised me with the $64,000 question about what the people in the plants thought of him. I could have copped out and remained quiet, but I did my best to be helpful.

I carefully but candidly related how the workers could not understand why he rarely visited their plants. Thus, they felt he didn't care about them. What I thought would be a five-minute interview lasted almost an hour. Although I didn't want to offend him, my honest evaluation seemed to impress him very much.

I heard later that he began to visit the plants more

often and eventually became more highly regarded by the employees. About a month after starting my new job, I had an opportunity to speak privately with my new superior. He told me that he was a good friend of my previous boss, who had chided him for hiring away "one of our best engineers."

Ten years later, my original company recruited me to "return to the fold" as a corporate engineering director. I was surprised later to learn that my return came about because my $64,000-questioner had recommended that the company attempt to rehire me any time a suitable position became available. He never forgot my honesty.

—*Lesson learned*: Avoid burning the bridge behind you, because that bridge might be your way back home!

A Lovely Day
Matt McMahon

My mother, Mary, always loved a party, so her upcoming ninetieth birthday provided me with the perfect occasion for staging a celebration in her honor. Mom, a victim of Alzheimer's disease, was a resident of Lovely Lake Nursing Home.

Athough Mom's memory had failed, I felt certain she would be able to seize the moment and enjoy the festivities. With the cooperation of the home's staff, I invited everyone on Mom's floor to attend.

I planned a simple affair with ice cream, cake, soft drinks, coffee, and tea. I would "headline" the entertainment by singing along with old Mitch Miller tapes. I was sixty years old, not bad-looking and an experienced singer. What my singing lacked in quality, I knew I could make up for with enthusiasm and infectious good humor.

On the big day, I arrived early and found the hallway outside the assembly room lined with wheelchairs of ladies waiting to go to the party. Gosh! I thought, only a few years ago these women must have been a lot of fun. And I was pleased I had a chance to bring a little joy into their lives.

The staff had prettied them up for the occasion with

makeup, and some of them even sported new hairdos. Many wore party dresses that I was amazed they still possessed. I quickly went about getting the tape player going while attendants wheeled the ladies into the room. Mom was already there, sitting behind a big frosted cake with "Happy Birthday Mary" emblazoned across the top. I sensed her enjoyment of the unfolding excitement as she dipped a thin finger into the frosting and listened as Mitch Miller's boys strummed tattered memory strings.

Soon wheel-to-wheel, the guests circled the room and the partygoers, feeling the excitement, responded with smiles, humming, and even some soft singing that delightfully surprised me. Attendants and nurses, leaning on the walls and watching through the doors, smiled and sang along as my wife and sister cut the cake and prepared to serve the ice cream.

If you lived at Lovely Lake, Mom's party was the place to be on that Sunday afternoon. With visiting rooms quiet, it provided an oasis in time for faded prom girls, many of whom old acquaintances did forget. I sang for them and serenaded the cheerleaders I had never met, but wished I had known. I even hugged a few, hoping that they remembered love. I won't forget eyes lighting up throughout the room to the harmonies of Mitch's chorus singing "When Irish Eyes are Smiling" and will fondly remember coy, almost embarrassed smiles as I strolled about the room, occasionaly stopping to hold a few hands, while singing along with "My Girl's an Irish Girl."

As I moved among the circled wheelchairs, I felt the whisper of a touch on my backside. Was it a chair rolling into me? I wondered. Or maybe it was an inadvertent arm brushing my rear attempting to retrieve dropped cake? No! I realized as I turned and caught the grinning eyes of the guilty "pincher." I always knew that some girls had more fun than others!

I continued to sing as the guests ate cake. "I didn't get any," one trickster with frosting on her chin complained. I gave her a second piece and another hug just in case she forgot my first hug, too.

The nurses reported later that one woman spoke for the first time in months. Mom, with a broad smile on her face, fell asleep halfway through the party.

It was, indeed, a lovely day at Lovely Lake.

—*Lesson learned*: I was reminded of the lyrics from a song by Strauss: "The golden moments swiftly pass—we must enjoy them while we may."

Let Me Count the Ways
Author Unknown (submitted by Marjorie Free)

I've learned that hugging is nothing less than a miracle:

Hugging is healthy:
- It helps the body's immune system.
- It cures depression.
- It reduces stress.
- It induces sleep.
- It is invigorating.
- It is rejuvenating.
- It has no unpleasant side effects.

Hugging is all-natural:
- It is organic.
- It is naturally sweet.
- No pesticides.
- No preservatives.
- Absolutely no artificial ingredients.

Hugging is practically perfect:
- There are no moveable parts.
- No batteries to wear out.
- No periodic check-ups.
- It has low energy consumption.

- It has high energy yield.
- It is inflation-proof.
- It is non-fattening.
- No monthly payments.
- No insurance requirement.
- It is theft-proof.
- It is non-taxable.
- It is non-polluting.

. . . And, of course, it is fully returnable.

How Wisdom Comes

Hoh Indian Elder Leila Fisher
(as told to Steve Wall and Harvey Arden)

Did you ever wonder how wisdom comes?

There was a man, a postman here on the [Hoh Indian] reservation, who heard some of the Elders talking about receiving objects that bring great power. He didn't know much about such things, but he thought to himself that it would be a wonderful thing if he could receive such an object—which can only be bestowed by the Creator.

In particular, he heard from the Elders that the highest such object a person can receive is an eagle feather. He decided that was the one for him. If he could just receive an eagle feather he would have all the power and wisdom and prestige he desired. But he knew he couldn't buy one and he couldn't ask anyone to give him one. It just had to come to him somehow by the Creator's will.

Day after day he went around looking for an eagle feather. He figured one would come his way if he just kept his eyes open. It got so he thought of nothing else. That eagle feather occupied his thoughts from sunup to sundown. Weeks passed, then months, then years. Every day the postman did his rounds, always looking for that eagle feather—looking just as hard as he could. He paid no attention to his family or friends. He just kept his mind fixed on that eagle feather. But it never seemed to come. He started to grow old, but still no feather. Finally, he came to realize that no matter how hard he looked he was no closer to getting the feather than he had been the day he started.

One day he took a break by the side of the road. He got out of his little Jeep mail-carrier and had a talk with the Creator. He said, "I'm so tired of looking for that eagle feather. Maybe I'm not supposed to get one. I've spent all my life thinking about that feather. I've hardly given a thought to my family and friends. All I cared about was that feather, and now life has just about passed me by. I've missed out on a lot of good things. Well, I'm giving up the search. I'm going to stop looking for that feather and start living. Maybe I have time enough left to make it up to my family and friends. Forgive me for the way I have conducted my life."

Then—and only then—a great peace came into him. He suddenly felt better inside than he had in all these years. Just as he finished his talk with the Creator and started getting back into his Jeep, he was surprised by a shadow passing over him. Holding his hands over his eyes, he looked up into the sky and saw, high above, a great bird flying over. Almost instantly it disappeared. Then he saw something floating down ever so lightly on the breeze—a beautiful tail feather. It was his eagle feather! He realized that the feather had come not a single moment before he had stopped searching and made his peace with the Creator.

He finally learned that wisdom comes only when you stop looking for it and start truly living the life the Creator intended for you.

That postman is still alive and he's a changed person. People come to him for wisdom and he shares everything he knows.

[—*Lesson learned:*] Even though now he has the power and the prestige he searched for, he no longer cares about such things. He's concerned about others, not himself. So now you know how wisdom comes.

MEET OUR 50-PLUS WRITERS

Charlotte Adelsperger is an author and speaker from
Overland Park, Kansas. She coauthored with her daughter
Karen Hayse a gift book for mothers, *Through the Generations:
The Unique Call of Motherhood*. In addition to softball, she
loves to play tennis and to hike with her husband, Bob.
(*See pages 28–29.*)

Helen Troisi Arney's elegy to her husband, "Holding
Hands," has appeared in publications including the
Chicago Tribune magazine, *Reader's Digest*, and *A Second Chicken
Soup for the Woman's Soul*. She writes the "Widowed Walk"
column for a biweekly newspaper and has written several
novels. (*See pages 10–12.*)

Jim Atkins is a general assignment reporter for the *Lake
Worth* [Florida] *Herald*. He also writes a weekly column
on topics ranging from politics to humor. He has written
two joke books and has worked in many political cam-
paigns. His advice: get a guru and drink wheat grass
juice. (*See pages 87–88.*)

Lauren Bacall was born in Brooklyn. She was off to
Hollywood at nineteen and a movie star before her
twenty-first birthday. A role model and romantic heroine,

she is a two-time Tony Award–winning actress whose celebrity only increases with time. She won the National Book Award for her internationally best-selling memoir. *(See pages 65–67.)*

Shirley Barksdale is a freelance writer living in Highland Ranch, Colorado. Her credits include *Reader's Digest, McCall's, Chicken Soup for the Soul,* and *Guideposts,* among other publications. *(See pages 103–105, 175–177.)*

Nova N. Barnett is now retired and resides in Titusville, Florida. She is an artist and an author. Her latest novel, *The Urn,* appears on 1stbooks.com. *(See pages 167–169.)*

Bill Bartell, a retired magazine and newspaper freelancer, is a native of Illinois and served with the Infantry in World War II. *(See pages 81–83.)*

Lee Berk was shot in the chest during the Battle of the Bulge on Christmas Day, 1944. He spent twenty-five years in women's wear (no jokes, please!), then went back to accounting. He writes children's stories under the title of "Grandpa Berk Stories." In his words, his most memorable achievement was "a very happy marriage." *(See pages 78–79, 112–114.)*

Catherine Berra Bleem, R.N. (retired), is an elementary school volunteer. She lives on a historic site in southern

Illinois. She is married, mother of five, grandmother to eleven, and "Granny B" to almost all the children at Central School. *(See pages 50–52.)*

Mary Bordan was employed for several years in the space program and later operated her own secretarial service. Now retired, she resides in Palm Bay, Florida, with her husband of forty-five years. *(See pages 20–22.)*

Laurie Boulton has had her work published in numerous publications and has won awards for nonfiction short stories, essays, and poems. She specializes in photo-illustrated rhyming verse poems for and about veterans. She self-published a book, *Heart to Heart Poetry for Veterans*, which she distributes free. *(See pages 36–37, 155–156.)*

Virginia Brodin, retired nursing supervisor since 1979, lives on a golf course outside Escondido, California. She loves travel both in the U.S. and abroad—and loves golf anywhere. She has four children, two grandchildren and two great-granddaughters. *(See pages 94–95.)*

Marian Brovero is fortunate in that she is able to divide her time between the sunshine of Florida and the beauty of the New Jersey shore. She tries through her writings and her volunteering to lend a caring heart to children and their parents. *(See pages 124–126.)*

Marlene Brown lives in New Canaan, Connecticut. She is an avid tennis player and enjoys weekly sessions of T'ai Chi instruction. (*See pages 162–164.*)

Peggy Bruce, a retired postal worker, lives in Clearwater, Florida with her husband, Garry, also retired. They have two children and three grandchildren. (*See pages 142–143.*)

Lillian Jane Cook, mother and grandmother, was widowed after sixty-three years of marriage. She was president of the Columbus and Topeka, Kansas, Federation of Women's Clubs and was state historian for the organization. She worked eleven years for the IRS, and is proud of work she has done tutorig uneducated individuals to read. (*See pages 17–19.*)

Carole J. Cosentino is an aspiring writer/late bloomer, now coming of age. She lives in East Rutherford, New Jersey, with husband, Tom (retired). They are parents of four and have three grandchildren. Carole is a senior citizen advocate. Stories from the heart are reflected in her writing. (*See pages 70–72.*)

Mary C. Dannettell has retired from forty years of teaching Physical Education. Having also majored in history, she now spends time giving talks on the local history of Evansville, Indiana. She continues working in genealogy and is an antique dealer. (*See pages 68–69.*)

Dixie Darr is an independent writer, teacher, and life-long learner. She lives and works in the Highland neighborhood of Denver, Colorado. (*See pages 178–180.*)

Dolores A. Dietz of Tinley Park, Illinois, a recent widow, is the proud mother of six sons. She has always had a desire to write about the happy and funny experiences she and her husband had raising their youngsters. (*See pages 53–54, 92–93.*)

Leila Fisher is a Native American elder, and Indian "Wisdomkeeper," who lives on the Hoh Reservation in the state of Washington. (*See pages 211–213.*)

Marjorie Free is semi-retired: she works three days a week and plays four. She lives in Portland, Oregon, eighty miles from the ocean (where she plays), enjoys cross-country skiing in the Mt. Hood area, and rides the ferries out of Seattle. She considers herself blessed. (*See pages 8–9.*)

Sharon Gagne is a physical therapist at a Veterans Administration Medical Center. She lives in Wappingers Falls, New York, and has three children and one brand-new granddaughter. (*See pages 137–138.*)

Margaret Kahn Garaway, eighty-three, the mother of three sons, has nine grandchildren and three great-grandchildren. She lives in Tucson, Arizona, with husband, Martin; is a publisher; and has authored five children's books. Margaret currently advises budding authors, speaking at schools and to adult groups. (*See pages 188–190.*)

Dorothy Girling resides in Escalon, California. She is a great-grandmother, an award-winning artist and past correspondent. Her volunteer activites have included 4-H, Cub Scouts, American Cancer Society, art guilds, and women's clubs. Some of her art has helped various organizations as fundraisers. (*See pages 106–107.*)

Frances golden is one of our over-eighty writers. She worked as a beautician, and later earned her Bachelor of Music Education degree. (*See pages 200–202.*)

Reverend Billy Graham is one of those rare individuals who has become a legend in his own lifetime. He has been called the world's best-loved evangelist. One educator said of him: "His genius for satisfying a hungry soul is unmatched. (*See pages 45–46.*)

Grace Lee Groves still lives on the family farm. She has been a lifelong homemaker and a caregiver at the hospital for fifteen years. (*See pages 59–60.*)

Mitzie Ann Hankins has ten grandchildren who keep her "forever young." She and her attorney husband, John, live in Huntington, West Virginia. (*See pages 56–58.*)

Mary M. Harper, an avid genealogist for thirty years, enjoys writing about her childhood and family. She and her husband have been married over forty years and have two sons and one granddaughter. (*See pages* 146–147.)

Rita M. Haun, a retired discount store assistant manager, is an avid reader and gardener. She dabbles in acrylic painting and is a lifelong "wanna-be" writer. She is a widowed grandmother of ten. (*See pages* 5–7.)

Norman Heberer, a consultant living in Augusta, Georgia, retired after working forty-one years as an engineer in the pulp and paper industry. (*See pages* 203–205.)

Ellen Javernick is a writer and first grade teacher from Loveland, Colorado. She's "Grams" to Ally, three, and Katie, one. (*See pages* 144–145.)

Lanie Johnson is a former commercial artist who has been traveling since 1995 in a truck camper throughout the Western United States with her husband, Ken Fischman, while observing, doing artwork, and learning more about life. (*See pages* 33–35.)

Tony Jones, of Whitby, Ontario, Canada, is a master athlete who has done it all: walking, running, biking, weightlifting, golf, javelin, swimming, you name it!

"I will never lose the will to live," he says, "When I'm at discotheques, I reverse my age digits from 81 to 18." (*See pages 31–32.*)

Ruth Jung lives in Chester, Illinois. She is a retired nursing home adminstrator and has survived both heart bypass and cancer surgery. She keeps active with volunteer work and enjoying her grandchildren. (*See pages 150–152.*)

Elyse Kaner holds a Master's degree in Curriculum and Instruction. She taught choral music for twenty-five years and is now enjoying her second dual career as a reflexologist and writer/reporter for a Minneapolis suburban newspaper. (*See pages 172–174.*)

Barbara A. Kiger, a tansplanted Michigander, lives in Tallahassee, Florida. A wife, mother, and grandmother, her writing reflects the multidimensional aspects of her life. Wait long enough, her family says, and you will find yourself in one of Mom's stories. (*See pages 15–16.*)

Nina Kluger, a former music student and bookkeeper in the New York area, now loves to write for her own enjoyment. She and her late husband had been married fifty-one years. (*See pages 170–171.*)

Steven J. "Bud" Lesko, Jr. is a retired college instructor and engineer. He was a lieutenant in the U.S. Army during World War II and was married to a wonderful lady for fifty-one happy years. He has nine grandchildren and four great-grandchildren. He presently volunteers as a student advisor. *(See pages 165–166.)*

Dr. Jeffrey LaCroix practices veterinarian medicine in Wilmington, North Carolina. *(See pages 97–99.)*

Bard Lindeman, a career journalist, is the author of *Be an Outrageous Older Man*. He lives in Stone Mountian, Georgia. *(See pages 128–130, 193–195.)*

Kitty Marbury, proud mother of two and grandmother of three, is a "semi-retired" hairdresser. At the age of seventy-eight she still gardens and is very active in her church. She lives in Baton Rouge, Louisiana. *(See pages 13–14.)*

Peggy Marteney and her husband, Gordon, retired from Oceanside, New York, to Wellington, Florida. They have three children and one granddaughter. *(See pages 43–44.)*

Mary H. McAllister, eighty, of Titusville, Florida, is the widow of Rev. Vernon McAllister, Baptist Pastor of central Florida. She retired after nineteen years as a teacher of special education in the public school system of Polk County. She is the mother of four children including one now deceased. Her hobby? "PEOPLE!" *(See pages 157–158.)*

Feliciana O. McClead is a seventy-plusser living in Florida. She has been married forty-five years, and has two children and three grandchildren. (*See page 89.*)

Matt McMahon, a retired scientist, lives in Wappingers Falls, New York, with his wife Carole. He participates in musical theater and community affairs and likes writing for the enjoyment of others. Both he an Carole play golf and they travel to three different states to visit children and grandchildren. (*See pages 206–208.*)

Krystyna Mernyk retired as a Registered Nurse after forty years of service. She lives in Sleepy Hollow, New York, with her husband. Both enjoy life to the fullest. (*See pages 25–26.*)

Jean Moyer retired after twenty-seven years as a teacher and lives near Sturgis, Michigan. She and her husband, Wendell, spend their winters in Destin, Florida. She is a writer, an avid reader, a quilter, and devoted grandmother of five-year-old Tara. (*See pages 41, 62–64, 101, 153, 183.*)

Barbara Oeffner and her husband, Thom, reside in Moore Haven, Florida, where they own a call center. She has just completed her Master's degree in Library and Information Science at Florida State University as a distance learner over the Internet. (*See pages 38–40.*)

MEET OUR 50-PLUS WRITERS

Stephen Press has had a lifelong love affair with the theater. He recently directed *The 1940s Radio Hour* for the Dutchess Community Colleges (New York) Masquer's Guild. The production was part of a commemoration of the veterans of World War II. *(See pages 115–116.)*

Jane Ritter, a lively seventy-six-year-old great-grandmother resides in Dallas. She is upbeat despite major surgery and a recent stroke. Among current projects she is writing a book of stories about her ancestors dating from the Civil War up to the Korean War, in which her MIA jet pilot husband was shot down. *(See pages 121–123.)*

Katherine Runyan and her husband, Ed, live in Melbourne, Florida. Retired from bookkeeping, she makes daily obeisance to her computer. She denies Medicare eligibility (but admits that Ed has rushed her to the emergency entrance of her beauty salon). *(See pages 108–109.)*

Deborah R. Sackel, a retired personnel manager, lives in Poughkeepsie, New York, with her husband, Joe, and three cats. Debbie, a member of Motor Maids, Inc., and the American Motorcycle Association, enjoys riding her two Harley-Davidsons. *(See pages 131–133.)*

Shelley Peterman Schwarz is an award-winning writer and contributing writer to *A Second Chicken Soup for the Woman's Soul*. She's also a professional motivational speaker and author of five books, including *Blooming Where You're Planted: Stories from the Heart*. (*See pages 148–149.*)

Lori Selby-Dailey has happily married again and is now living in Melbourne, Florida, where she spends her time reading and playing tennis and bridge. Her only "claim to fame," other than this contribution, is the fact that she was one of the original Washington Redskin Cheerleaders. (*See pages 119–120.*)

Shirley Thompson lives in Indian Harbour Beach, Florida, near her three daughters and two marvelous grandchildren. (She also boasts about her granddog, Sunny.) Her favorite pastime is writing stories for her grandchildren. (*See pages 139–141.*)

Phyllis G. Tritsch resides in Melbourne, Florida. She is the retired EVP of American Women in Radio and Television, and is both a Certified Fund Raising Executive and a Certified Association Executive. Her articles on fundraising and association management have appeared in various professional journals. (*See pages 117–118, 134–136.*)

Jean Vaughan is a widowed mother of three children and grandmother of five wonderful grandchildren. She also is and has been an aspiring writer since she had an article published in her high school newspaper many years ago. (*See pages* 23–24.)

Sidney Wallach lives in Buffalo, New York, where he is chairman of a manufacturing company. He worked for the *Herald-Tribune* in Paris, the *St. Louis Post-Dispatch* and the American Broadcasting Company. (*See pages* 85–86.)

Ron Wiggins is a popular columnist for the *Palm Beach Post*, West Palm Beach, Florida. His versatile writing talent allows him to cover a wide range of subjects from the deadly serious to the delightfully humorous. (*See pages* 159–161.)

Ruth Wirth is a retired teacher of thirty-seven years (including thirty-plus years in special education) in Colorado, Illinois, and Arizona. She is the mother of two sons, grandmother of six, and great-grandmother of nine. She enjoys cooking, writing, painting, and sewing. She and her husband, Jack, have been married for forty-eight years. (*See pages* 47–49.)

PERMISSIONS

❧